THE TOP MANAGER

PROVEN TOOLS & MINDSET TO **LEAD** WITH AN EDGE

MADOU SYLLA

www.TheTopManager.com

Copyright © 2013 MADOU SYLLA

ISBN: 978-0-615-85100-6

Printed in the United States.

HOW TO

READ

THIS BOOK:

The MAIN objective of this book is to transform you into a management powerhouse capable of creating ultimate business success. You will master the psychology required to become effective and influential in any environment. This book is broken down into four sections and each serves a specific purpose to help an average leader become a TOP MANAGER.

SECTION 1:
ACQUIRE THE MINDSET OF A TOP MANAGER:

It is impossible to become an effective leader without acquiring a strategic mindset and developing the required emotional toughness when leading people. This section covers **15 directives** that will put you on a platform that breeds **respect, responsibilities, results, excitement, control, authority, and excellence** .

SECTION 2:
MASTER THE BUSINESS ANALYSIS:

Every leader will face tough challenges that demand action. To fix any problem, you first must be able to define it clearly. This section covers **12 CRITICAL ANALYSIS TOOLS** you must assimilate to determine how your systems, strategies, and resources are performing on a daily basis. To ensure that the reader gets through this book with ease, the sections that require more in-depth analyses and financial calculations were moved to the Appendix Section. You should definitely cover those sections at some point since they are not difficult to understand and apply.

SECTION 3:
BUILD THE BEST STRUCTURE:

Without developing an effective and efficient organizational structure, you have little chance of being profitable long-term. This section outlines in detail, a proven business model you can implement to become not only, highly efficient but also positioned to increase consistently your performance and productivity levels.

SECTION 4:
OPTIMIZE FOR ULTIMATE EFFICIENCY:

Specific business systems require more attention in an organization. This section covers **11 Critical Business Systems** a leader must prioritize for continued profitability and long-term sustainability.

APPENDIX:
The appendix covers three areas in the Business Analysis section that require a deeper analysis and calculations:

- The Comparative Cost Analysis
- The Z-Score Analysis
- The Optimum Break-Even Analysis

QUIZ:
Once you finish covering the four sections outlined above, you are encouraged to take the Top Manager's Quiz. It will help you measure your progress and the milestones you have reached in regards to the learning objectives.

40
COMPETENCIES
TO HELP YOU
SOAR TO THE TOP

TABLE OF CONTENTS

GOALS &

OBJECTIVES

Is it easy to catch a monkey in the jungle?

Would you consider moving to an uninhabitable place if you were promised endless wealth?

If your eyeballs could shoot balls of fires, would you use this unusual gift given the potential risks?

The three questions asked above may seem totally bizarre and unrelated. However, they epitomize the barriers preventing average managers from becoming great. They are: Uncertainties, Hard Choices, and Fears. Let's find out...

Well, how can one catch a monkey in the jungle? If you are not in the business of catching monkeys in jungles, then it is likely you can't fathom how difficult it is even for the most advanced hunters. No one has yet been able to come up with a rock solid strategy that works every time. Every scheme, strategy, or trap ever developed has had its shares of disappointments and shortcomings. However, by consensus, most monkey hunters would agree that it takes unwavering patience and dedication. Just like an old proverb states: *"Slowly, that is how you catch a monkey in the jungle..."*

As a leader, they are simply things you do not know, will not know, and will not care to know about. That is normal. The expertise required to catch a monkey is something you may never have to put to use. Therefore, who cares? However, you may still agree that the attributes required to catch a monkey which are patience and dedication are essential to any successful leader. So, should every leader learn how to catch a monkey? The answer is no. As regular human beings, we cannot possibly know everything and master every skill in one lifetime. Many things will always remain a mystery to us.

However, here is the big question: Can we create constant success despite our ignorance in so many areas? Or, will the uncertainties we have prevent us from developing winning agendas in all of our endeavors?

Secondly, the average person does not wake up one day and decide to move to a place that is unfit to live unless strong motives such as wealth or love were part of the decision-making process. However, billions of people rise every day with hopes of generating wealth. It is difficult and only a select few have done it. Most end up giving up on wealth to seek only a paycheck that will provide for their basic needs. If all the wealth you were seeking, is given to you with the condition that you must live in a place that most of us are only content to read about in geography books, would you do it? Ultimately, being wealthy is great if you live around people? A castle made of gold is not as precious if you are the only person to enjoy it or see it. However, if wealth is something you always wanted, then you have do it? Or, is wealth what you were always seeking?

Hard choices are destined to come upon us. The big question especially for a leader is: Will the right choice be made?

And finally, would you light places on fire just because you could? Or, would this gift stay dormant and never utilized because your common sense tells you it's too risky. The prospect of starting a devastating wild fire, or turning a city with millions of inhabitants into ruins may be enough to convince you to not use this gift. You may fear the outcome of your actions even if you contemplate lighting only small targets on fire. However, it is still a cool gift and your deep curiosity wants you to go for it.

Unless you can look into the future, you will fear the consequences of the "tough" decisions you have to make.

The question is: Can you manage your fears effectively when these decisions have to be made?

The questions above represent the torments many managers are faced with on a daily basis. Obstacles and difficult decisions have and will remain ongoing elements of the business environment. With the multitude of uncertainties, hard choices, and fears facing leaders of all backgrounds, many will often haphazardly employ a broad range of erratic strategies without the assurance that they will result in the desired outcomes. Essentially, the likelihood of business success becomes a game of odds and chances, equating to the hazards of playing the lottery.

Understandably, 85% of new businesses will file for bankruptcy within their first seven years of operation. The next 10% remain engaged in fierce battles just to stay afloat financially. Unfortunately, only about 5% of businesses possess the winning game plan needed to generate a handsome return with the assurance of long-term sustainability.

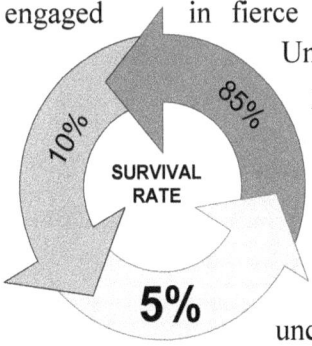

85%
10%
SURVIVAL RATE
5%

This begs the question: Is it possible to become a very successful leader despite uncertainties, hard choices, and fears. The answer is YES ... and it is simple. You have to become the Top Manager. It's more than a title; it is the personification of ultimate excellence—*delivering decisive success without everything that is ruthless and painful about running a business*. It is about amplifying the effectiveness of choices and decisions. Abandoning all desires to follow the norms. Being courageous regardless of circumstances. And above all, developing emotional and intellectual toughness.

The Top Manager operates in a different dimension, running effortlessly on water and walking painlessly on fire. This book is not a feel-good, self-help exercise in self-esteem; it is a clear-cut collection of decisive measures that has helped Top Managers of all backgrounds. Simply knowing the concepts discussed herein is not enough to lift one up to the level of Top Manager; it is about activating these demonstrated principles in the right proportions … to find the recipe that yields managerial magic. This book will guide you in how to attain that ultimate leadership competency.

BRACE YOURSELF! You are about to master the requisite tools to become a true Game-Changer. In short, this book will help you unleash the Top Manager within:

- Guessing Business Strategies – Forget it
- Prisoner To Uncertainties – Certainly Not
- Chaotic Business Environment – Eliminated
- Bad Business Decisions – Nevermore
- Leading People – Easy
- Team Atmosphere – Superior
- Competitive Forces – No Problem
- Generating Consistent Profits – Effortless

The tools utilized by some of the best managers in the world will be at your disposal. With time, patience, and dedication, they will become like second nature. You will have the managerial acumen necessary to deliver optimum results for any company.

By immersing yourself in the proven strategies covered throughout this book, you will become the force that drives the business forward, the herald of success, and savior to the stakeholders. Instead of allowing a business to shut its doors and terminate employees, the Top Manager leads an organization to victory. The workers keep their salaries, and families continue to prosper. In like manner, a community will thrive because you manage a very profitable company in its territory.

THE BOTTOM LINE:

You will learn a systematic approach that will help you conquer those tough business challenges that the average business leader dreads. In the end, you will accomplish the following:

- You will learn to cut through the clutter and push through with an effective agenda
- You will master the psychological prowess required to get your team to trust you and follow your leadership with enthusiasm, dedication and loyalty
- The status quo will no longer apply because you will have the ability to develop winning strategies in all of your endeavors

HERE WE GO...

SECTION I –

ACQUIRE THE MINDSET OF THE TOP MANAGER

MINDSET

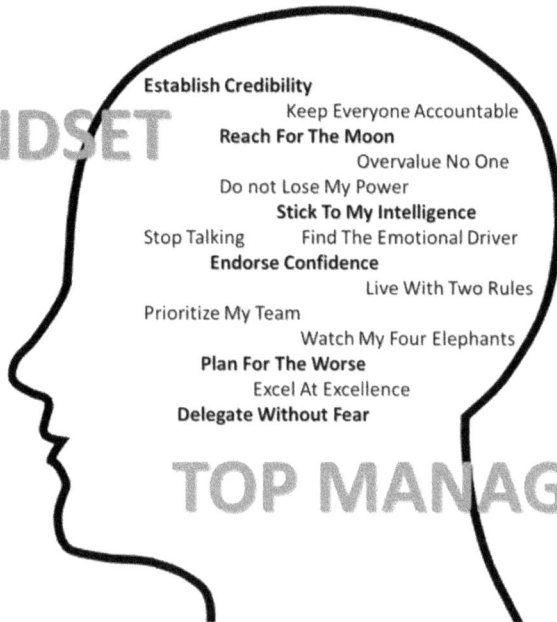

Establish Credibility
Keep Everyone Accountable
Reach For The Moon
Overvalue No One
Do not Lose My Power
Stick To My Intelligence
Stop Talking   Find The Emotional Driver
Endorse Confidence
Live With Two Rules
Prioritize My Team
Watch My Four Elephants
Plan For The Worse
Excel At Excellence
Delegate Without Fear

TOP MANAGER

First and foremost, you must accept that effective leadership stems from the psychological prowess of the Top Manager. Accordingly, your primary goal is to use the skills outlined in this book to prioritize your management directives. The central theme of your management style should be your push to create a unique and fertile environment that inspires contribution and collaboration. Part of being the Top Manager is in possessing a commanding presence. This will enable you to lead people along the designated path of success.

The basic pillars of effective management can be well summarized in two words: **CONTROL AND AUTHORITY.** Failing to secure these two prerequisites as the foundation of your leadership platform will leave you impotent to achieve your goals, consistently frustrated and unable to influence the state of mind of those you lead.

Throughout our careers, many of us are instilled with the notion that Control and Authority are leadership characteristics that create a sour work environment. Dismiss these thoughts immediately. Having *control* equates to the ability to inspire cooperation amongst those you lead. And when your words carry *authority*, your directives will hold the validity needed to get things done.

To illustrate the mistake of the negative connotations, consider a manager who retains *control* over his team through the threat of punishment or rebuke. A manager who loses his temper when workers make mistakes. Employees have no carrot, and only fear the stick. Compliance with managerial mandates is compulsory. This manager is neither admired nor respected. Superficial compliance is acquired through negative reinforcement. There may be some semblance of coerced *control*, but it comes without any true *authority*. Employees in this environment follow the letter of the law, but not of the spirit. Without true Authority, this manager will never compel his employees' best efforts. In the context of the Top Manager, control is in fact the by-product of authority.

So what is *authority*? It is more than a position and a job title. It is more than having the corner office and a dedicated parking spot. It is more than employees scrambling to look busy when you enter the office. It is more than barking orders and micromanaging. True authority certainly extends beyond. Authority delegates, and remains in the air even when you are not around. No "cat's away, mice will play" type of atmosphere. Authority is exemplified by the Top Manager's ability to inspire the team. The innate skill to gain voluntary cooperation is one of the Top Manager's most important attributes. Master these concepts, and your employees will display genuine deference while in your presence.

The Top Manager must take on a sort of tactical persona. Let us disavow any nefarious associations we have with control, authority, tactics, or strategy when it comes to superior/subordinate relationships. These need not be adversarial to be effective. One can employ tact and strategy without being inherently manipulative. While engineering situations may be necessary to convince your employees to work toward a common goal, it does not necessarily mean you are being dishonest or unscrupulous.

Consider it an inevitable necessity to accomplish the goals and objectives of your organization. Let's refer to it as: "The Top Manager's Game Face".

HERE IS THE RATIONALE:

As a manager, you do or will work directly with many people with different backgrounds, personalities, and belief systems. This is inevitable throughout your career path. You will work with accountants, mid-level managers, customer service representatives, IT professionals, support staff, administrative, sales professionals, and about everyone in between. This diverse group of people, backgrounds, personalities, and skill sets all come with different opinions, methods, and ideas as to how things should be done. These opinions all have origins as diverse as the company's labor force itself. The actions of different people in your organization are derived from a disparate set of perspectives and motives, both personal *and* professional. The Top Manager not only recognizes this, but tailors actions to address this aspect of the work environment.

The tactics of the average, undiversified manager do not address the absence of homogeneity. People hold on to idealized notions of equality, with the premise being that "everyone should be treated the same." Most people however, are completely satisfied as long as they do not feel as though they are being treated worse than anyone else is. The Top Manager intuitively knows how and when to employ different managerial tactics to get the desired results. This must be done subtly. The Top Manager realizes that a one-size-fits-all approach is grossly ineffective, and constantly seeks ways to motivate different individuals to respond to managerial directives.

Different people have different motives. From a simple and fundamental professional perspective, we can all appreciate why the interests of salaried, hourly, and commission-based employees may not always be aligned. The same goes for the various career ambitions held by each member of the team. Any effective management style must be able to adapt to this varied atmosphere. The Top Manager will seek to create an environment and framework of systems and controls that will have these different objectives working in sync with one another.

Personal motives are even more diverse than career oriented ones. These may include a desire for recognition, a congenial working atmosphere, a flexible schedule, vacation time, or constructive workplace challenges. Regardless of the individual situation, the Top Manager must be attuned to the different things that make certain individuals tick, and respond accordingly.

Without acquiring this tactical mindset, the average manager reaps what he/she sows: an environment with the following characteristics:

- Constant confusion
- Disinterest in organizational success
- Lack of productive participation
- Uncreative environment
- Lack of personal responsibility

There is no doubt you have heard the age-old adage for computing – "garbage in; garbage out". Yes, your employees may "take your orders" because of the position you hold. However, can you earn their trust and respect? Will they follow your leadership enthusiastically? If your management style is, for example, "garbage", there is no doubt that the manner in which employees carry out your plan of action will result in more of the same. Conversely, *authority* found in the Top Manager's leadership prowess will inspire enthusiastic cooperation, and *control* will not be forced or coerced. This is the hallmark of a truly effective boss.

The following **FIFTEEN CONCEPTS** will help you not only secure control and authority with those you lead, but also master the mindset of a Top Manager:

1.1. ESTABLISH INITIAL CREDIBILITY:
You have a small window of opportunity to shine.

Let's assume that you are the owner of a small company with twenty employees. You are very ambitious and have been dreaming for something bigger. Hence, in the past few years, you have been pushing for an aggressive growth initiative. You have dedicated a considerable amount of your time writing business plans and meeting with investors. Finally, the day comes when you catch your break and secure the investment you have been wanting.

However, the investment comes with one condition; the newly created business must be located in a place that is essentially, uninhabited. This place is far away, cold, and so desolate that no one with a free will could possibly want to visit it or even live in it. You quickly recognize that in order to make this new dream a reality, you must take your employees with you. Now, your next challenge is to convince twenty people to leave their families behind and everything they know and love to follow you to the other end of the world.

Will they do it? Probably not and the reason is simple...

People will not follow you to the end of the world if you are an average person (leader). Why will they do it? Why will they turn their lives upside down just for the sake of a paycheck? Most, if not all, will take their chances in their local job market instead of venturing out into another galaxy. Perhaps if they believed that you were extraordinary, they may look beyond the sacrifices they have to make and get on your train. They wouldn't want to desert you because in their minds, you always accomplish extraordinary things and everything you do makes sense and is warranted.

So, when does the process of seeming extraordinary in the eyes of others begin? **Answer:** Right away... **on the first interaction**.

When you first meet people in the professional world, they will consciously and subconsciously be looking to determine your level of credibility. Your coworkers, colleagues, superiors, employees, and partners will instantly begin to form an estimation of you and your capabilities, for better or worse. Do you deserve your position? Are you as talented and qualified as your resume reads? Are you capable of delivering great feats? In other words, they will be "sizing you up". Like it or not, you are constantly being evaluated. In most cases, people will generally formulate an initial opinion about you within two to three minutes of interacting with you. First impressions only take a moment to take shape. A bad first impression is usually impossible to repair.

Within moments of entering into a conversation, people may decide that you are a complete idiot, or the greatest person they have ever met, and anything else in between. In essence, you do not have months or years to establish credibility. From the standpoint of social interaction, this perceived credibility is developed instantaneously. It is natural for human beings to make judgments and assessments of others in social and professional situations. Often this involves looking for faults, whether real or perceived. Even the smallest faux pas can unravel your credibility like an old sweater. All you need to give is one loose thread.

Without realizing it, you will be fighting a losing battle if your mannerisms and habits wreck your "first impression" from the onset. This is particularly crucial when considering your interaction with new staff members over whom you preside. Your credibility is inextricably linked to your authority, and by extension, your ability to exercise control. Making the right first impression is crucial. Let's classify this initial interaction as the "Opening Conference". It is during this opening conference, and especially during the first few minutes of interaction, that your credibility will be established.

THE IMPORTANCE:

Establishing credibility among people with whom you will work is very critical to your leadership role and the aspirations you have; your ultimate success depends on it. The average person will not go the extra mile for you if they believe you lack the expertise and ability to deliver extraordinary results when necessary. Your personal competency, business acumen, and validity of leadership are under constant scrutiny from those you manage. Do not doubt that these people will test you to see what you are made of. Establishing credibility must be firm, swift, and decisive. Simply because no one should question who holds the role of Top Manager. Even scarier, many people will **unconsciously** "size you up" on the initial interaction. This happens because their brains are constantly working and even if they have no opinion of you after the first interaction; their subconscious may have developed some type of classification in regards to what type of person you are. When the time comes, this cataloguing may come back from nowhere to convince people they shouldn't follow you to the end of the world. You are just like everyone they have met and therefore not deserving of any special treatment. You are just a regular run-of-the-mill earth dweller and you are far from being earth shattering.

Strategy:

Next time you meet people, behave as if you may ask them at some point to follow you to the end of the world. You will realize how much of an attitude change you will need.

SO HOW DO YOU ESTABLISH INITIAL CREDIBILITY?

First, What Not to Do…

1.1.1. TOUTING YOUR EXPERIENCE:

It is unnecessary to brag.

"Can everyone hear me: I am the best"

People, especially the more sophisticated ones, will not be impressed with what you have done for Company X or Y six months ago; or even the milestones you have reached throughout your "long and illustrious" career. As far as people are concerned, you very well could be exaggerating the facts. In fact, most recruiters and hiring managers worth their salt will assume this to be the case to some degree. It is an unspoken rule that "enhancing" the facts is common practice. For this reason, statements like "started the most profitable company in the southeast" or "went IPO within three years" begin to lose meaning. You can't rest on your laurels. Expecting past achievements to garner you instant credibility is like deciding to drive a car blindfolded because you have done it so many times.

Let's say you don't take this advice to heart. At your opening conference, you dive into an in-depth dissertation of your achievements. It's highly likely that you've just given the impression that you are an egotistical, self-absorbed, arrogant person. It is counterintuitive, because people enjoy talking about themselves. The Top Manager knows when to show restraint. Besides, people are usually apprehensive when they hear exceptional stories, as immediate proof is usually not available. Self-aggrandizing war stories about the amazing feats you once accomplished are also not helpful. It is almost reminiscent of a panhandling vagrant wearing a sleeveless business suit and camping boots who regales any sympathetic ear with past successes and triumphs of the "good old days". The Top Manager only needs to rely on current results.

As a Top Manager, you can never be viewed as a salesperson. This may go against the grain in some regards, as the conventional knowledge surrounding professional development focuses heavily on "personal branding" and selling your "image". Career coaches, recruiters, job placement centers, and resume tip books all advise people to have crafted and rehearsed an "elevator pitch". As a Top Manager, this concept should make you shudder. It should make you squeamish at the thought of ever delivering one, and agitated that someone should expect you to have the patience to deliver the same. In this context, the classic elevator pitch is less about demonstrating value, and more geared toward how many buzzwords you can pack into a 30-second self-absorbed distortion of the facts.

Generally speaking, people can tell when you are being disingenuous. We do not consciously realize it, but our brains are processing an immense amount of information at each moment throughout the day. Our brains conduct thousands of calculations per second on a subconscious level. This is the same reason why without realizing it, people prefer symmetrical faces to those that are not. It is why structures with precise mathematical angles and proportions are pleasing to the eye. In addition, it is the same reason we get a "feeling" that someone is lying, exaggerating, or withholding elements of the truth. It is because we are picking up on a variety of non-verbal cues that we have learned throughout a lifetime of listening to "salespeople" managers boast about how they singlehandedly tripled revenues at their previous job, all while performing the job duties of three people. This does not mean everyone is a liar. To put it another way; a used car salesperson can tell you how great and reliable a car is, but his word is no substitute for taking that same vehicle on a cross-country trip. This is the same rationale behind avoiding the sales-pitch personal introduction. In fact, you shouldn't have to "pitch" yourself at all. Your attitude, demeanor, and emotional intelligence should do this for you. Past achievements and work experience should simply serve as a supplement to your commanding presence, not as the foundation upon which your credibility is based.

From a strategic point of view, selling yourself and your achievements will only impress average people who can't help you climb the ladder of success. These people have not achieved anything significant and for this reason may glare with admiration once, you start elaborating on your resume. And that's where it stops. The more accomplished people who could possibly expand your horizons can do it because they too, have achieved great things and have opened many doors. Elaborating on your triumphs will not convince them to work with you. You simply run the risk of aggravating them and totally writing you off after the first interaction. To impress this group of people, you have to **demonstrate intellectual and emotional toughness.**

1.1.2. RAMBLING ON ABOUT YOUR EDUCATION:
Your Training is Personal and that's it.

Formal education is a tradition. The more you pay for it, the more prestigious it is viewed. Listing an Ivy League school on your resume will kick down doors that are closed to most, and will impress many people who have a traditional mindset toward a business education. Odds are, if you are in a corporate management position, you probably have a reasonably good education from a reputable institution of higher learning. If you went to a good school, this is something you certainly want to highlight. It is something you should cherish. However, you should never make it a central point in your opening conference. Your education must never define who you are. It is another attribute of the professional package that comprises your managerial persona. However, the degree you hang on the wall of your office is never going to roll its sleeves up and do your work for you. Your education says something about who you are, but your actions speak volumes.

You must realize that your formal education is a personal achievement, and not indicative of your true abilities. An education is nothing to boast about, no matter how exclusive the university. Think for a moment, about your fellow students … even the ones in the most advanced courses you took during your college or post-graduate experience. It is almost a certainty that a minimum of one or two of these people were complete wastes of their parents' tuition money. Now imagine these same individuals, after graduation, bragging to colleagues, coworkers, prospective employers, clients, or even subordinate employees about where they went to school. So how much value is it fair to place on an education? Ceteris Paribus, anyone who heard the both of you discuss your alma mater would have no choice to assume the two of you were cut from the same cloth. That is not to say that there is no value in a prestigious education. It also does not mean you shouldn't be proud of your hard work. But let others come to that conclusion on their own. The Top Manager has no reason to brag. This is the sign of an emotionally insecure person. The Top Manager let's actions speak louder than words. Others will do the bragging on his behalf. Likewise, an education should speak for itself, and require little unsolicited clarification. It is therefore unnecessary to elaborate upon without outside inquiry, especially during a first interaction. People don't like to listen to others talk about themselves. If people want to know, it's likely they will ask you. Besides, getting your education is something you did in the past. The various stakeholders of your new environment, i.e., the business you work for, should be more worried about what you are going to do in your current role. Remember, your Opening Conference is about getting to know the people with whom you will work. If you make your education a main premise of your value proposition, you run the risk of initiating a sales-pitch type interaction. As we discussed, this is immediately harmful to your credibility meter.

1.1.3. THE TYPE OF MANAGER YOU ARE:
Where is the current proof that you can deliver?

The same concepts as outlined above also apply here. To put it bluntly, don't talk about it, be about it. If you have ever been the person in charge of reviewing applicants for an important position, there's no doubt you've seen your fair share of resumes. After looking over just a few, you might be impressed by someone who lists a collection of impressive accomplishments and achievements. After you've looked over several dozens, you start to realize that everyone does this. All resumes begin to look like the same old tired, slightly modified, worked over, and chewed up regurgitations of one another. They all use nearly identical phrases like "proficient at multi-tasking" or "work well in a collaborative team environment". You then become embarrassed thinking of all the times you wrote similar rubbish early on in your career.

The unfortunate part is that it is not these peoples' fault. They are groomed and conditioned to present themselves in this fashion. Truly, only about one in a hundred resumes you come across is dynamic, concise, well written, and original. The rest could almost be photocopies with the name changed at the top. The same goes for the way people speak about their prior work experience in an opening conference. This lack of originality is betrayed by the lack of conviction that accompanies one's use of another's words. Rigid responses characterized by more inquiry in their inflection than the question to which they are directed.

Their self-assessment often involves a blundered coalescence of clichés and buzzwords. If you have the dubious experience of working in an environment that treasures staff meetings, it is likely you've witnessed the jargon contest once or twice. The next time you find yourself in this setting, ask yourself if opening your mouth will really contribute to the dialogue, or whether you are really speaking to emphasize your attendance. It almost seems as though the people saying these words and phrases are not even sure if they know what they mean. However, it's usually okay; nobody else does either ... or at least no one is certain enough to call them out on it. Either way, it is not an effective approach by which to portray the type of manager you are. People will follow a natural leader. Leaders lead by action, not jargon.

Even more damaging than rambling off a banal collection of managerial platitudes is when you just start telling people how great you are as potential co-worker with nothing to back it up. As a general strategy, you must always avoid divulging too much information about yourself that is not easily verified. You may be the best manager on the face of the earth, but people have to work with you before they can make their own conclusion. People will not take these claims at face value ... they are simply claims until direct experience can prove otherwise. So why not let your actions speak for you? Remember, you should not appear as though you are interviewing for a job when you first meet people, even when you are. Therefore, it is ill advised to engage in any conversation that may lead people to doubt the accuracy of your statements.

1.1.4. YOUR RUSH EXCITEMENT TO WORK WITH PEOPLE:
Early enthusiasm is absurd.

Enthusiasm can indeed be contagious. Insincere enthusiasm is like a cancer. People can always tell. It will kill your credibility. It may sound counterintuitive, but you should avoid giving praise and positivity to people during the initial interaction. Not only is enthusiasm viewed with skepticism when it comes too soon, but why should you be so enthusiastic before you've even gotten a chance to know what the relationship will be like? Worse yet, unbridled excitement has nowhere to go but DOWN. For all intents and purposes, the competence level of those you first meet is ambiguous. And that's the best case scenario. In most cases, you will know little to nothing about these people, beyond perhaps a resume, a recommendation, or through a networking event.

People will be left wondering why you are so eager, even if only subconsciously. You are essentially giving accolades to them before they have proven their value. Would you tell a blind date you look forward to marrying them? No, you know far too little about their character and compatibility. Would you tell the doctor getting ready to perform a complicated brain surgery on your elderly parent that you have already written a letter of recommendation for her? Of course not, and you can only wish that she has steady hands. You have to approach simply these types of situations with a cautious optimism. To do otherwise diminishes your credibility. One can easily discern why this would be the same with a new work environment. Never gush during an Opening Conference. Clients will think you have something up your sleeve. Bosses will think you're kissing you know what. Employees will think you're going too far to ingratiate yourself. Most will know that you are insincere.

Employees who work only for the paycheck already approach these interactions with skepticism, and will think you're full of something other than exhilaration. All of these groups will secretly be amused by your statement, because you have completely misdiagnosed them. Your credibility is instantly in question, as you are demonstrating ignorance by uttering nonsense and unverified praise.

SO, HOW DO YOU ESTABLISH CREDIBILITY IN THE EYES OF THOSE YOU MANAGE?

Hands down, you have to be the undisputed expert in your environment. Being "the expert" does not mean you know everything. In fact, being an expert means you know just enough to ask the right questions. Everybody despises a "know-it-all". Be ready to defer to your team. The simple gesture of asking what someone else thinks gains you an immense amount of respect and credibility.

ASK QUESTIONS, ASK SOME MORE, AND ASK AGAIN.

Whether it's your first day overseeing an already established group of employees or a new team member has just joined your staff, it is important that your authority is credible from the onset. Without sounding cliché or arrogant, they must "know who's the boss." To do this, you have to earn respect. This is only done legitimately through demonstrating your knowledge and proficiency; by showing, you have earned the right to occupy the spot of "Top Manager".

Get your employees involved with your vision and accustomed to your way of doing things. Engage them in a thoughtful and serious conversation about your expectations of them, their job duties and perhaps even how to install specific systems and controls. Offer your insight when a clear answer is lacking. Offer praise for critical thinking. Seek their input when there is a shortage of good ideas. Be sure to demonstrate that you possess the expertise to address every situation, and make it clear how you expect tasks to be implemented in the future. You have to keep your staff sharp, alert, and responsive to the challenges they face throughout their workday, week, month, and year.

What do we mean here? Let's say you just started a new manufacturing company. You saw a great opportunity to provide a certain product. You knew you could source the materials, machinery, capital, and talent needed to provide and produce at a very competitive price. You get the operation set up and ready to go. The machines are in place, customer contacts have been made, and your first truckload of raw materials arrives next week. You realize your first challenge is going to be hiring a qualified VP of Operations. This is one of your more important hires, because this highly visible position will control much of the workflow and the manner in which things are done. You have to be certain that the person you choose to fill this role will take his fiduciary duty seriously. The most crucial part of this role will not just be carrying out your orders, but carrying out the duties of the job as you intended. You want a highly competent, knowledgeable, and capable person to fill this position. At some point, you may even need to ask this person to follow you to the end of the world. However, your past experience has shown you that these individuals are also often the most difficult to manage. As you have probably experienced, smart people don't always do well taking orders. That is why your status as Top Manager must be unimpeachable from the first meeting. If you are viewed as softhearted, weak, or too forgiving from the onset, the coming months will be fraught with confrontation and complex situations.

Now fast forward to hiring day. Things are up and running, it's Monday morning, and the top candidate on your interview shortlist comes in for one final meeting. Everything looked great on paper, sounded good on the phone, and went smooth during the first interview.

But you want one more face-to-face before starting the work relationship officially. "Good morning, Eddie", you say in a pleasant yet serious voice. Eddie moves toward the two chairs in front of your desk, lays his briefcase on the chair next to him, takes a sip of his coffee, and asks about your weekend while removing his jacket. At this point, he is trying to feel you out. Maybe he is trying to cultivate a friendship relationship to protect his position. Time for the "Opening Conference".

Your focus here is to give Eddie a reason to respect your leadership. If this dynamic is absent, your ability to lead your VP and those he manages will be seriously compromised. One misstep and things will only deteriorate from here. But you know better, because you have at your disposal all of the tools and strategies used by the Top Manager.

Therefore, you expertly go about establishing your credibility ... Here is how the Top Managers do it:

"My weekend was fine," you reply. "Have a seat. Let's talk. Have you had a chance to look over the operational analysis I sent you on Friday?"

You know that he hasn't. There is no way he could have. It would have taken you more than two weekends to review them, and you wrote them. But you want to knock him off balance just a little bit. Not to be brutish or mean spirited, but just enough to earn the upper hand early in the conversation.

"I glanced through them, and think I have a pretty good idea of where we're going," he says.

"Well then," you reply, "how do you suppose we should go about determining which one of these product lines is going to be most profitable? Which one should we launch first? And what should be our rollout plan"

This is a very tough question for anyone to answer without performing an in-depth financial and market analysis. Accordingly, Eddie's very first answer to you should be "I don't know."

At this point, your credibility meter is moving up, and it will increase progressively as you remain consistent with targeted questions. Eddie should be sitting up by now. Maybe he's even adjusting his necktie. He is quickly realizing that this first meeting is going to be very serious. If Eddie hazards a guess at your question, and stumbles through a half-baked response about profit margins and market research, you quickly respond with a poignant yet calm targeted question:

"Okay Eddie, so you are telling me that you would be willing to guess without conducting financial projections and a thorough market analysis?"

Now perhaps you feel that using a "trick question" is disingenuous. Perhaps your initial inclination is to view this as manipulative or dishonest. But remember, all is fair in love and war. Business is a type of war. War with external factors, war with clients, war with the bottom line. A constant competition, and a struggle to gain ground, not to lose it. Your goal is to come out victorious. And you want to be backed by a loyal group of soldiers. You need to test Eddie's loyalty along with his business acumen. How can you send him into battle without making sure he's ready?

You are not making Eddie feel uneasy just for the sake of it, but more trying to guide his emotional state toward wondering why he would have been so presumptuous with his response. In military boot camp, the drill sergeant's primary duty is to break down the new recruits before they're built back up. In this Opening

Conference, you are like a drill sergeant, just a quieter version. Remember to be decisive with your actions, austere with your words, yet tactful with your approach. People respect the Top Manager because he has it together. This is crucial to laying a solid foundation to any managerial platform.

Another good question to ask might be "So Eddie, How did you develop production standards, systems, and controls in your last role?"

If he can answer with ease, then you are in a good position because you won't have to spend your busy days training this employee. If answering this question is difficult, then Eddie will be forced to say, "I don't know", again. Either way, you are in a great position. Through targeted questioning, you are progressively demonstrating your own expertise, and thus establishing credibility.

Remember, everyone you manage will have their own distinct set of skills, their own strengths, and their own weaknesses. People try to cover up the latter, but you must probe to find them out. Everyone, regardless of how smart or talented, will have some type of deficiency in at least one subject matter or skill. This is universally unavoidable. The Top Manager knows how to buttress these deficiencies and emphasize strengths. A well-chosen team is able to complement one another. Team members should help one another fill in the gaps. Your squad needs to be seamless and air tight.

So now, you have to figure out if your new candidate for VP of Operations is going to fit well into the fabric of your organization. Your basic strategy in the opening conference is to find Eddie's strengths and weaknesses. Ask questions. Ask many questions. Write them down beforehand and be more than adequately prepared. Once you've confronted him with a barrage of questions to test his strengths and weaknesses, you've not only found out vital information about this employee; you've also demonstrated why you are in the Top Manager position.

The above scenario obviously does not take into account the multitude of ways in which your questions could be answered. The fact of the matter is, it does not matter how Eddie responds to your targeted questioning. Your fundamental approach is to always focus the conversation on the field that concerns this VP. Whether or not he can answer your questions with ease is irrelevant. You will have accomplished your main goal, which is to demonstrate that you are only interested about the matters that are the most important in the Eddie's role. You might go on to ask your new recruit several more questions. As you can tell, these are very targeted:

- How will you separate direct costs from overhead?
- How will you departmentalize financial statements by departments and units?
- How will you implement capital & operating budgets?
- What type of cyclical inventory system do you suggest for our operations?
- What systems will you use for an effective accounts receivable program?
- What quality control standards and functions would you install?
- What reports will you have available to ease management's decision-making process?
- How will you calculate optimum Break-Even points?
- How would you implement optimum distribution channels?
- What do you believe should be the optimum equipment level?
- What should be our optimum number of locations?
- How will you calculate the optimum volume for our operating level?
- What pricing structures and strategies can you implement?
- What cost control programs can you implement?
- What should be the basis for our emergency cash management system?

- What system should be in place for our capital acquisition program?
- What should be our market-positioning strategy?
- What diversification model do you suggest for long-term sustainability?
- What type of industry analysis can you conduct?
- What should be our contingency plan to sustain our company in case of a recession?
- What strategy do you suggest for cross-selling & value-added opportunities?

The thing to remember here is you are not talking about the moon landing, curing cancer, global warming, starving children. You are making a straightforward and relevant statement with this "interrogation". With a consistent bombardment of targeted questioning, Eddie quickly understands the depth of command you must possess in these critical business practices. **In essence, asking the right questions makes you an expert by default.** The best part? You never had to prove you know anything. You never made any declarative statement. Lastly, always ask follow-up questions. If you ask questions to your employees and they respond aloofly with "I don't know", then your follow up question should be "Why don't you know?" This will force them to acknowledge their limitations. From a psychological standpoint, this is a very powerful tool. Generally speaking, people usually respect those to whom they admit their shortcomings. If done correctly, your new VP of Operations will not care about what you have done in the past or where you went to school. It will be the furthest thing from his mind. This VP will simply accept that you are a credible leader; **your interests are in line with managing the organization, not promoting your own self-image.** To your benefit, this sentiment is everything you should expect from an employee.

1.2. KEEP EVERYONE ACCOUNTABLE:

Optimum execution at all times... is the norm.

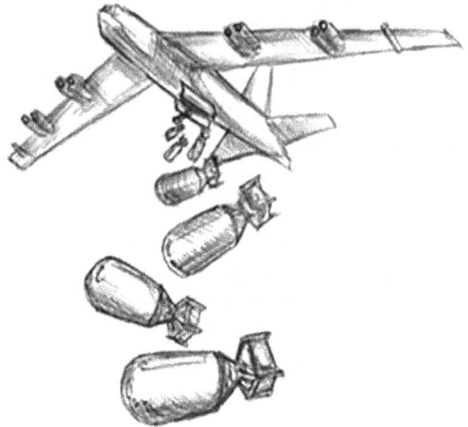

"Well if it rains today, at least I will be prepared"

After a successful "Opening Conference", it is time to begin a working relationship with your newly hired employees. Throughout the course of these relationships, you will come to share many experiences with your team. You will get to know them intimately on a professional level. You will have the chance to analyze their work and actions closely. If you pay attention, you will gain useful insight as to how they work, what makes them tick, and what you need to do to manage them effectively. Every time you determine an employee has fallen short in a specific task, then you should point it out immediately. Hold them to task. Everyone is accountable, and **every transgression will be dealt with swiftly**.

As a Top Manager though, you can never hesitate to confront your employees. You should always point out deficiencies and errors for the sake of a positive outcome. You need to let your employees know when they are not performing up to par. How else will they know what to correct? Polite society abhors confrontation, and anything that resembles this immediately becomes a violation of acceptable decorum. Disregard this convention. If you walk on eggshells too often, you're bound to get little pieces stuck in your feet. You need to be very clear about what is bothering you.

The best way to confront people is to establish a laser focus on the target. It may even throw them off balance. This is fine, as it will probably open a more honest line of communication in both directions. This should in no way be considered harsh. Confronting people is necessary for a number of reasons. If done tactfully, this may even inspire an employee to go above and beyond. Negative feedback can be appreciated when properly delivered. Accountability is true honesty. It gives the employee an opportunity to improve in areas where they may be lacking. This practice is far better than the ineffectual nature of the manager who wishes to avoid what he feels is "confrontational". The nervous manager's displeasure for unsatisfactory performance will shine through, despite an attempt to avoid confrontation. It will come off as passive aggressive behavior, and will likely generate a rift between boss and employee. This is counterproductive to fostering a successful team environment, and is usually detrimental to managerial credibility. Conversely, bringing your concerns to an employee in a stern but respectful manner is always the best approach. This does not mean that when taking corrective action, a manager needs to coddle the employee. There is no place for "kid gloves" in the repertoire of the Top Manager.

Sometimes, a regular confrontation does not always get the job done. Time to raise the volume. The louder it is, the more the damage. The ultimate confrontation is letting someone go. At this point, the individual is beyond help. However, it will send a loud and clear message to everyone else. When serious mistakes are made, they must be met with appropriate intensity to emphasize the urgent need to make changes. Besides improving business operations, the purpose behind catching employees off guard is to challenge any notion that questions the Top Manager's authority. Making it a standard procedure to consistently confront everyone is by far one of the most successful methods to keep employees alert when they perform their job duties. The Top Manager will be able to gain organization-wide support for his directives. He will able to communicate his vision to the team. He knows that members of this team may have great ideas to improve frontline efficiency, and is able to acknowledge and implement these improvements without damaging his own credibility. He will not however, allow the employees to think that they can operate at will.

THE IMPORTANCE:

An organization filled with complacent employees winds up rife with debilitating inefficiencies. When too comfortable, these workers may become careless in performing tasks. If the company lacks strong leadership, complacent workers may feel they have no consequences to face for sloppy work performance. Your company will find itself constantly putting out fires, fixing mistakes, and doing the same task twice to get it right. Negligence and hasty work can lead to significant problems in the long and short term. Measure twice, cut once.

"Legal policy errors" are the best ones to emphasize because they are accentuated with the seriousness factor. Let's assume for example that you are reviewing a new employee's file. In this file, there is usually a job application form, identifications documents, tax papers, etc. Let's also assume that your organization has a zero-tolerance policy against sexual harassment. For this reason, every new employee is made aware of the policy on the first day of work and must sign a document stating that the policy is understood and will be followed. Once signed, this document is added to the employee's file. Let's also assume that in this particular employee file you are reviewing, the sexual harassment policy file is missing. Accordingly, you've just uncovered a clear blunder from the Human Resources Director.

How should you confront the HR. Director? Start with this question:

"Do you know how much the average settlement on a sexual harassment case is?" As she is thinking or says, "I don't know", you reply "$450,000". You then continue to explain …

I was just reviewing the new employee's file and couldn't find the signed sexual harassment policy document. Here is our problem: Do you know that when a sexual harassment claim is filed against an organization, the first basis for potential judgment for the court is to determine if the organization in question has done enough to prevent sexual harassment? They will first start by verifying our employees' files to substantiate if there is an active policy signed and understood by the staff in question. If this policy is missing in our employees' files, then the court could conclude that we don't have a policy and technically, permitting sexual harassment in our organization.

Something as simple as one piece of paper read to and signed by employees can be the difference between a "guilty" or a not "guilty" verdict. Not considering the potential embarrassment our company may face from the publicity of a lawsuit and court proceedings, do you think we have an allocated sum of $450,000 sitting in our bank account waiting to be paid out to a sexual harassment claimant?

Your explanation may be followed by a long pause; you wait for the response: "… no". Before you hear any excuses, walk away!

The reason why it is psychologically important to not allow the employee to give you an excuse of why this fault was committed is that you don't want this issue to be resolved immediately.

Think about this for a moment...When people make a mistake and apologize, and you accept it, the offense may be forgotten in a few days. It is considered resolved. You don't want that. When a serious breach of protocol occurs, it needs to remain in the air for as long as possible. Let this uneasy silence become your ally. You want to ensure that next time the HR. Director will create an employee file; the sexual harassment policy will be prioritized.

Without doubt, this treatment may be considered blunt. However, it's necessary to emphasize an imperative point, and spur immediate change when addressing very serious matters within an organization.

It is important to acknowledge that as you are confronting people, your credibility meter will gradually increase. However, you should employ care. Avoid beleaguering petty items that have no perceived gravity from the employee's perspective. By all means, refrain from dropping them with malice. Doing so will actually harm your credibility. You then run the risk of being viewed as being overly concerned with details. Nitpicking unnecessarily may put a dent on the credibility you have already built.

1.3. OVERVALUE NO ONE:

No one is Special and everyone is Replaceable.

"Why do I get the feeling that today is going to be a bad day?"

In some organizations, it is common practice for a certain group of people to receive special treatment. These are the people top-level managers will usually stay away from because of extraordinary reasons. For instance, nepotism could have put a family friend or blood relative in a position which their skills or background do not warrant. Even worse, perhaps the company is holding on to otherwise "problem employees" because they do one task particularly well or have the desired expertise in a field. Either way, the presence of such employees poses a distinct challenge. Let's call them the "sacred cows". Even if these "sacred cows" engage in unproductive behaviors, everyone will turn a blind eye because of their perceived importance.

Extending special privileges to select employees is a terrible practice; Everyone in the organization should receive comparably equitable treatment and operate under a uniform set of rules. Every single employee must understand that no one is special and everyone is replaceable.

1.4. DO NOT LOSE YOUR POWER:

Without a license, you can't drive freely.

"C-c-can we settle this over a c-c-cup of coffee??"

Take the example of a person named Emily. Throughout her career, Emily has held several managerial positions in different organizations. One day, she receives a very exciting phone call. A board member of a large organization contacts her to interview for a CEO position that just became vacant. She is being considered because she has excelled everywhere she has been and many influential people are praising her abilities. Without delay, she is interviewed and lands the job. Emily joins this new company with great excitement and is eager to make her mark right away.

She spends the next few months analyzing the company's products, marketing strategy, sales strategy, operational resources, market opportunities, etc. Basically, she looked under every single rock. After this intensive and thorough process, it hits her. Eureka! She has it all figured out. Emily then drafts a comprehensive plan she believes will turn her new organization into a profit-making machine. Her plan includes a complete turnaround of the company's direction by offering new products, opening new supply chains, and going after markets everyone previously considered impossible. She is overcome with excitement. Very excited and ready to go. However, her job contract clearly states that she must get the board's approval before undertaking any major project or changing the company's direction. In her thinking, "No big deal. This is a genius plan. They will love it".

It is now time to present this plan to the board members and of course, she knocks it out of the park. After she finishes her presentation, she is told: "Very Good. We will talk this over and give you an answer within a week". The week goes by fast and she is back in front of the board to hear their decision. To her surprise, it's a simple no. What can Emily do? Nothing.

A problem she didn't see coming...

From the onset, Emily failed to understand that good ideas and smart strategies are not enough. To do great things in an organization, one must first have the **POWER** to put them in action. Her first priority when she joined the new organization should have been to devise plans to diminish or eliminate the power the board has over her. She didn't understand that she was hired with limited authority. She spent months in the "zone" only thinking about profitability and efficiency rather than schemes to control her territory just like a dominant lion.

WHAT IS A DOMINANT LION?

A dominant lion has complete authority over his territory. His sovereignty is without question and his "scent" is present all over his land. Any potential challenger is dealt with swiftly without mercy.

LESSON TO BE LEARNED:

Emily should have realized right away that she had no real power. She just had a title and the territory she thought she controlled was non-existent.

If you have attained the top-level position in an organization, it is likely that your intellectual ability is above average. This means that at some point, you will probably have great ideas you would want to pursue. Not having the power to put them into action will make you essentially mediocre and borderline useless in comparison to the Top Manager. The moment you enter the premises of your organization, it should become your land. There are no areas in which your authority is to be questioned. No one should be able to force you into a position where your ideas and goals are subject to review and deliberation. Any successful manager needs power to accomplish big goals. Whether you started your own company or joined an existing one, never forget that your very **first priority is to establish your dominance, just like a lion in the wild.**

1.5. STICK TO YOUR INTELLIGENCE:
Wandering too much will get you lost.

As a Top Manager, you must trust and rely on your own aptitude and intelligence. Under no circumstances should you defer to the actions of other businesses. Never use a famous example to make a point about the positions you hold regarding your organization. If you must defend a specific position, be precise. Utilize your critical thinking ability to give clear examples. This is no time to color outside the lines. For example, stay away from clichés like Google, Wal-Mart, Starbucks, or Facebook to justify your opinions about operational decisions. Refrain from the business school's case study type of mentality. **It should be your turn to come up with something great for others to talk about.**

By pointing out where others have succeeded with a certain approach, you show that you are not an original thinker. Why should someone else's ideas have validity in connection with your company? It diminishes your credibility because your presentation does not include your intellectual prowess. You should also keep in mind that there will be people in your environment who are excellent debaters. If you base one of your arguments on the circumstance of another company, you may give them ammunition to contest your position. Consequently, you embolden people to challenge your intelligence.

If you open yourself up to hostile challenges and lose, you instantly damage your credibility. Even if your naysayers are wrong, you have still given them a forum in which to dispute your conclusions. What do you do? Fight or flight? You are now left with the unsavory choice of either engaging in back-and-forth quarrels or running for the hills and conceding your point. Either way, you won't come out smelling like roses. **The Top Manager's luster should never be tarnished.**

Instead, justify your ideas based on their own merit; not simply because you read about a new technique published in a credible business magazine. Fads thrive in the world of managerial concepts, frameworks, and theoretical tools. It is a popular move for weaker managers to latch on to someone else's ideas to increase their credibility and a sense of "being right". The Top Manager, however, has control of his own destiny. By explaining why your position is actually beneficial to the organization (as opposed to who else used a similar model), you get straight down to the point. This statement is debate free, because people can now only dispute the effectiveness of your position rather than point out differences between your organization and another.

1.6. STOP TALKING:

Chitchatting is useless and dangerous.

Once you establish yourself as the Top Manager, people may feel intimidated or nervous around you. This is a natural side effect of authority, but some of it must come from your own actions as well. As Top Manager, you are sharp, hold people accountable, and do not tolerate negative behaviors. In fact, there will be times when some may see you as an unemotional, straightforward, work machine who is only interested in *the business of the business for*

the business. This is because you take it to the next level when it's crunch time. Others misinterpret this if they lack your warrior instinct.

To ease the tension that exists around you, people will naturally start "small talk". They may initiate conversations about the weather, sports, the economy, world affairs, education, global warming, etc. You must be stern, disciplined and always give people the clear impression that you are not interested in that type of conversation. This is a natural response by employees seeking to ingratiate themselves with you. However, you are not here to make friends. In fact, doing so compromises your authority.

If idle chitchat persists, simply reply, "I would love to talk to you about sports (for example), but I have a lot of work ahead of me. Can we get back to the matter at hand?"

By now, you must be wondering why it is such a bad thing to engage in small talk with people. Perhaps you believe lighthearted dialogue and establishing common ground is beneficial to maintaining positive relationships with your employees. If people engage in "small talks" with you, it means that they are starting to like you. What's the big deal? Let's find out...

1.6.1. THE PERILS OF SMALL TALK:
It is matter of time before bad behaviors catch up to you.

Small talk is not about building relationships. It's not about relating to people. It serves little *useful* purpose beyond breaking an uneasy silence. Let that silence be your friend. It will certainly prove to be more useful in your business endeavors than engaging in conversation with little substantive value. Small talk is also gossip. Gossip is a weakness. A disease. It is contagious. There is no such thing as a secret, just common knowledge that isn't openly discussed. Gossip is a desire to know, or a compulsion to share information and feelings. Small talk is complaining. Indulging oneself in the act of telling other people what's bothering them. Small talk is an inflated sense of self-importance. Small talk is talking about people behind their backs. Gossip is the most egregious form of small talk, so it is clear why one would avoid this activity.

But, what about innocent chitchat? Certainly, that's innocuous enough, right? Wrong. Let's explore why ...

NORMALIZING FACTOR:

Engaging in small talk makes you a normal human being. A mere mortal in the eyes of your team. This is because personal conversations inadvertently reveal personal feelings, opinions, and beliefs without fail. It makes you more transparent and predictable. Once the small talkers begin to understand your psyche, they might conclude that you are just a normal human being after all! The moment you become normal, you become like everyone else—and not everyone is a Top Manager. Again, ask yourself the following question: Will people follow you to the end of the world if they believe you are a normal human being? The answer is of course "no".

As a Top Manager, everyone must think you can fly, shoot fire from your eyeballs, and walk on water. In essence, you must be seen as gifted. Always come to work as Superman; leave Clark Kent at home. Regular human beings are not gifted and therefore not worthy of being followed to the end of the Earth. If people believe that you are just like them, why should they put you on a higher pedestal?

RISK FACTOR:

Small talk can simply ruin relationships with people. Understandably, you can never make assumptions about people's beliefs systems, past experiences, general outlook on life, etc.; aside from the assumption that yours and theirs are bound to differ at some point. Opening up too much, especially on political, religious, or socio-economic topics, can expose you, and bring condemnation from those with whom you disagree. Once you go down this path, anything can happen. If you say something they vehemently disagree with, you can't un-ring the bell. Think you can keep things inside the boundaries? Think again ... who wants to listen to someone talking only about the weather?

TIME FACTOR:

If your employees are accustomed to engaging in small talk around you, then you may never get anything accomplished. Let us assume, for example, that your goal on a Tuesday morning is to start training your employees on an entirely new set of protocols for dealing with new projects. You spent the better part of Monday evening putting this together, because you've recognized a way to eliminate huge operational inefficiencies. You decide it's imperative that the new modus operandi be implemented immediately. Therefore, the goal is to get the training started and finished right away. You only have four hours to complete this training because you know you need to leave for a twelve o'clock lunch meeting. Either your employees can ready themselves for the scheduled training, or they can deviate to start talking about current events and national news. Sometimes people get comfortable putting off the big tasks by giving superficial attention to the matter at hand, or even worse, diverging into talking about their weekend, or the latest James Bond film in the theatre. You, on the other hand, acknowledge that the time you have as the Top Manager is very limited. You have many objectives to accomplish on a daily basis. Talking about new blockbuster releases is at the bottom of your list. Even worse, you don't want your employees to get the sense that they can pretend to "work" just by giving lip service to the important issues affecting your business. At all costs, it's time to avoid the conference meeting jargon contests. You should not allow anyone to waste your valuable time by engaging you in these sorts of useless conversations.

As a cohesive, functional, productive team, your employees need to work together seamlessly. This does NOT mean they deserve an extra hour spread across the day to regale one another about tales from their weekend.

To sum it up, the perceived benefit of engaging in small talk is negligible compared to the irreversible damage it may cause.

1.7. FIND THE EMOTIONAL DRIVER:
Focus on what makes a difference.

It is a fact that most people go to work just to earn a living: Paycheck to paycheck, 401k, two weeks off a year, a flexible spending account if they are lucky, and a nice medical plan through their employer. Emotional needs and personal motives are often buried amongst the need for economic survival. As the Top Manager, you need to find out what these personal factors are. It is important to know and understand people's drivers, as this is the key to being able to manage them more effectively. The driver is fundamentally the sentimental motive behind one's professional endeavors. In more specificity, why did someone choose to work at your company (besides the financial incentive of course)? If you've done your job right as Top Manager, the answer should not be "because this company is the only one that would hire them." People like this should never have made it past the front door in the first place.

Perhaps, an employee needed to prove to a family member that she could hold a job. Or, this person dreams of outperforming a college friend who is doing very well in her own career. Maybe this employee plans to learn all of your secrets and start a competing business. Even though finding the driver for each and every last one of your employees may prove next to impossible, you should at least try to uncover those hidden motives behind your immediate management team.

In strategic terms, finding this emotional connection attached to someone's career choice will allow you to target your managerial efforts more directly. Accordingly, you would be able to develop a systematic approach to increase their productivity once you have uncovered their ultimate driving force. The driver can sometimes be very difficult to ascertain. In some cases, it may be rooted deeply within a people's subconscious. They may not even know what it is or how it affects them emotionally. Even if this is the case, you still need to try. However, don't attempt to figure people out through small talk. You exercise restraint and caution in personal interactions. Again, be judicious as this may humanize you. Remember to be engaging enough without establishing too personal of a connection. Orchestrate "field tests" whereby you place employees in different scenarios to observe their reactions. These tests may give you a good starting point. Once the thread begins to unravel, keep pulling on it to expose their drivers. Now that you've figured out what makes your team tick you can structure better their job duties around the drivers. You'll soon find you've amplified their work output, because you've aligned their duties around their emotional connection to their position.

Let's assume that you uncover the driver of one of your most difficult to manage employees. You realize this person craves status, acknowledgement for achievement, and the ability to demonstrate to the outside world that she has "made it." Make her the person in charge on your next team project. Let this person know you are "counting on them" to lead the way. Giving orders will be extremely satisfying to her, even if it is a sort of pseudo authority. There is nothing wrong with pulling this driver out if you can use it to your own benefit. Better yet, you've delegated some day-to-day activities to free you up for big picture tasks.

THE STRATEGY AND THE RESULT:

1. If this employee thrives on giving out orders, she will be emotionally satisfied
2. If she wants to keep on giving out orders, her team will need to reach the established goals in order for her to keep her position
3. As a result, she will become a dedicated and hard-working employee because you have placed her where the emotional thirst is quenched

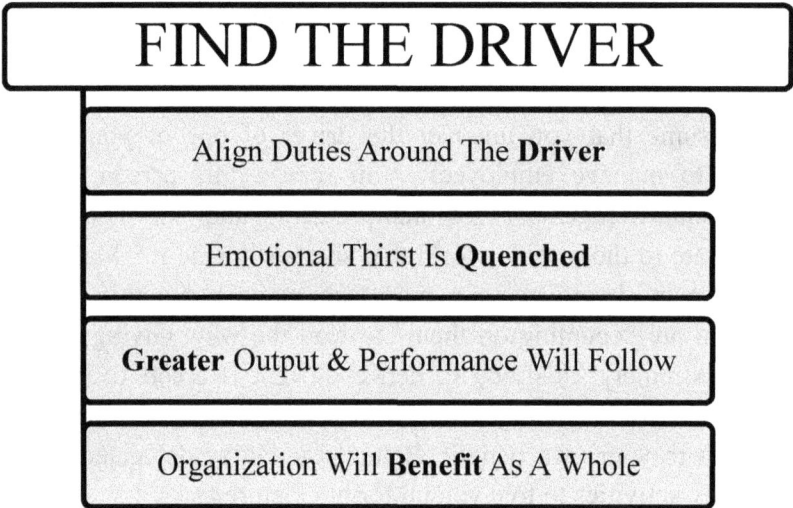

FIND THE DRIVER

Align Duties Around The **Driver**

Emotional Thirst Is **Quenched**

Greater Output & Performance Will Follow

Organization Will **Benefit** As A Whole

As a Top Manager, this is everything you should expect from an employee: Optimum productivity regardless of emotional drivers.

1.8. ENDORSE CONFIDENCE:

You are the smartest person in the room. Period.

"OK son, here is where you learn how to fly. Jump now…"

Growing up, your parents may have spent considerable time instilling you with the value and virtue of practicing humility in your everyday life. The honorable human being never makes excessive outward shows of confidence, unless he wishes to be perceived as arrogant … right? Perhaps this works for schoolteachers, librarians and museum curators, but tepid ambivalence and equivocation are not among the Top Manager's list of personal attributes. In the realm of the Top Manager, humility is a trait you shouldn't enormously value. You have to learn to prepare yourself mentally to exude the sense that you are the smartest person in the room, regardless of who is present.

You will probably not always be the smartest on all topics, but those around you must believe it. For you to achieve great success in any organization, it is essential for every employee to believe that you have the ability to deliver regardless of future contingencies. It is true that a fine line exists between arrogance and confidence. However, it is a risk you should always take. Simply put, the average person will believe only in those they consider smarter or more capable than themselves. By humbling yourself to that of an average mortal, you diminish your position. The average person does not command the same respect, as does the Top Manager. **Whenever people hear you speak, you should talk about big ideas and lofty goals**. You must use authoritative and powerful words. Everyone should believe that you are the common denominator to success and anybody in your camp will succeed.

WHAT MAKES MOST LEADERS SELF-EFFACING?

As is often the custom in bureaucratically predisposed organizations, many managers will work within a company over the course of several years while being promoted through the ranks by way of chronological seniority. These managers find themselves now in a position of control and authority through no extraordinary acts, outside of showing up for work every day and executing at the minimum level of acceptance. Once they get there, they will usually change little about the way they interact with those they now are leading. They will still behave as if everyone, including them, is on the same pedestal and no one is smarter than the other. A horizontal type of mentality that suggests that we are all the same and that extra confidence is not necessary.

These managers will likely be ill prepared to affect the sort of real and definitive change needed to lead an organization into the future, particularly if they are simply upholding a legacy of what has gotten them there—humble and average. They will replicate the status quo, stick to their comfort zone, and reactivate the same mindset they have used when they were just in the mix with everyone else.

Once the position at the very top is yours, you must swiftly transition your state of mind and prepare yourself to believe that you are the best at it and no one can do it better.

Ultimately, believing that you have the ability to do anything you want will dictate the objectives you seek and subsequently your achievements. If you believe that you are just like everyone else, then it is likely you won't seek to climb the highest mountains.

1.9. LIVE WITH TWO RULES:
A leader without a solid internal package has nothing to offer.

An effective leader must develop an environment where everyone is eager to help the organization achieve its goals. With the multitude of challenges an organization may face throughout the year, lack of meaningful employees' contributions should not be one of them. Once the right environment is established, the Top Manager will have no need to beg employees to perform up to par. They should willingly engage in battle on behalf of the company.

In order for the Top Manager to cultivate such an environment, he must possess Intellectual and Mental toughness. Let's demonstrate how critical these two concepts are to the Top Manager:

1.9.1. INTELLECTUAL TOUGHNESS:
An idiot cannot lead.

Simply put, you cannot get your employees to enthusiastically follow your leadership if they feel their expertise is beyond your own. The Top Manager can never be seen as one with a limited understanding of the organization, its key processes, or the actions needed to drive success. While the Top Manager surrounds himself with a management team comprised of bright individuals, he should never be seen as clueless. At a minimum, you must understand the critical aspects of the business just as well as anyone in the organization.

Here, we are not talking about mastering mundane tasks such as troubleshooting network server problems or fixing a jammed printer. There are people on the staff who are paid to know these things if you don't. We are referring to major items such as the business process requirements for the delivery of a product/service, strategy for approaching highly competitive markets, or the inefficiency symptoms. If people believe that you fully understand all of the critical elements of the business, then the decisions you make and the goals you set will not be subject to debate or ridicule.

Many dishonest self-help, feel-good business books have pushed this notion that we all can reach unparalleled success even with limited intelligence and abilities; all you need to do is follow the formula and utilize the strategies they preach in their teachings. They are simply misguiding people. Here we are not suggesting that your IQ score must be similar to that of Albert Einstein to become successful in business. However, we are saying that your intelligence level must at least be above average in order to face business challenges with a more strategic and tactful approach. The lack of intelligence of a leader is like going to war without a weapon. The odds of losing the battle are far greater than winning it. Furthermore, you have to prioritize the necessity of working toward mastering new skills each day. Don't be complacent and satisfied. Do something to educate yourself in a new field every week, read a good business book every month, or attend regularly *meaningful* management training seminars.

1.9.2. MENTAL TOUGHNESS:

Being calm under fire is a must.

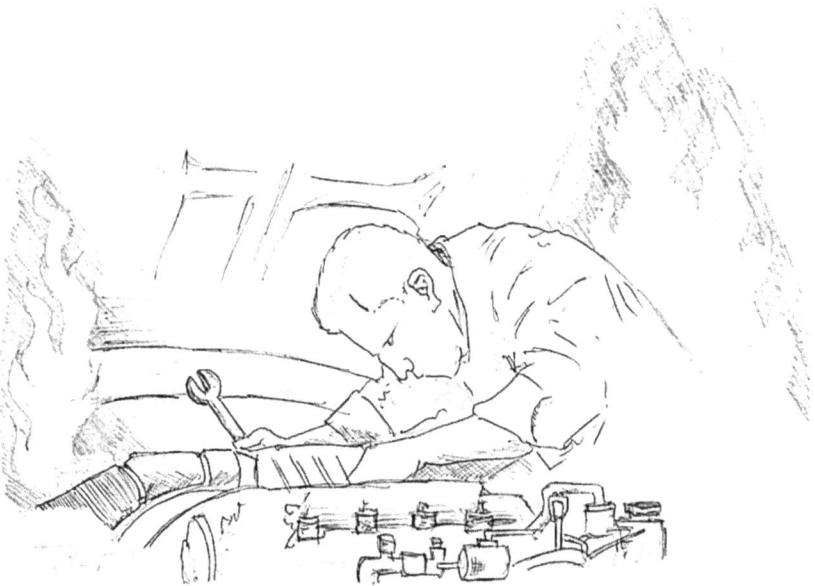

Mentally tough leaders are calm, collected, consistent in their demeanor, and always remain well poised. They are not rattled by difficult situations. They are the voice of hope during stressful situations. Any company can fall victim to difficult cycles. Slow growth, downturns, economic recessions, loss of profitability, external issues, changes in the regulatory environment and scandals are just some examples. Trying times require a leader who is mentally tough and who possesses the ability to navigate through the storm. A mentally tough leader is able to face down tough problems, brainstorm possible solutions, and move forward with an effective agenda. The Top Manager is able to do so with coolness, adept intuition, and never lets worry or concerns get in the way.

The Top Manager must be able to display decisiveness, thoroughness, and firm resolve for achieving success. People will respect and follow this type of leader because they know that any organizational crisis will be met with an effective approach. This leader is also the charismatic person everyone depends on to bring about a consensus, even when general disagreement is present within an organization.

On the other hand, we all have perhaps been around a leader who sought to display mental toughness by engaging in excessive emotional outbursts. Remember, as a general rule of thumb, a person who displays too many emotions during tough times is psychologically and mentally weak; unable to cope with the circumstances or to control the compulsion to show despair and anger. Mentally tough leaders are never too upset, never too excited, never too depressed and most importantly, are never hopeless. Whatever tangled situations arise, they know to stay composed and fix the problem. They take all of the factors into account, conduct a cost benefit analysis regarding the different alternatives, and swiftly take action to move forward accordingly.

1.10. PRIORITIZE YOUR TEAM:

Your team is your greatest ally to success.

Many companies tout a boastful tag line or adopt a mission statement to the effect that customers are their "number one priority". That is simply a foolish perspective to hold. Great companies prioritize their employees first. They understand that building an efficient team will ensure long-term growth and success. Instead of focusing solely on attracting the next customer, they will develop enhancement plans necessary to spur the innovative thinking ability of every employee. Customer satisfaction with supreme business service or offerings is sure to follow.

A Top Manager will dedicate a significant portion of his or her time to probing for skill deficiencies in employees, investigating outside seminars to train employees, taking part in the interview process of new hires, and setting up performance evaluation standards. In the eyes of inefficient leaders, these types of activities can always wait. In essence, they consistently fall into this dangerous trap of believing that more important issues require their immediate attention, and inevitably perpetuate the cycle of constantly needing to put out fires.

1.10.1. THE CARLA DILEMMA:
A diamond is precious and needs to be cherished.

Take for instance a receptionist named Carla. She works for a corporation with multiple layers of leadership. Carla is one of the lowest-paid employees in the organization because of a preconceived notion that her role in the organization is at best, minimal. The need for expert service at this level is viewed as unimportant, as the ineffectual manager views front-line positions as remedial. Furthermore, limited contact and interest from top-level managers renders her position more impotent, as a busy schedule and 'more pressing engagements' take precedence to mentoring 'lower level' employees like receptionists.

This viewpoint, however, is present in the most dysfunctional organizations. There is a pressing need in any successful organization to foster an environment of support and collaboration. This must be done from the ground up. Carla has in effect been disenfranchised insofar as the course of regular decision-making and contribution to the bottom line is concerned. Suggestions for improvement are not taken seriously, because after all, what would she know about running a company? To the contrary, front line employees are among the most important asset in a company.

LET'S DISCUSS WHY...

Carla will often be a given customer's first point of contact. Because Carla answers the phones and greets customers when they arrive at the company, she happens to be the most visible representative of the organization. Whether the customers get a positive or negative first impression of the company depends entirely on her performance. Let's say a prospective client had a dreadful interaction with Carla because she was too busy being unprofessional rather than welcoming a client. This client will undoubtedly have a terrible impression of the business as a whole, regardless of the company's proficiency in its professional endeavors.

On the other hand, even an organization with shoddy work practices and inept professional performance can fool a potential client into believing the company's work is rock solid – at least until it has delivered its work products! If the front line employees sell the customer on an impeccable professional image, the client may even be willing to overlook any negative experiences expressed by others. In this regard, even your front line administrative personnel are part of the organization's "extended sales force".

If the ineffectual manager decides it is beyond the scope of his responsibility to ensure that the receptionist receives excellent customer service training and direction, the bottom line will suffer. In Carla's case, her role is classified as less important, perhaps even expendable. Some may even justify this with the thought that eager replacements are easily found. With this misnomer at the front of poor management techniques and philosophies, many organizations ignore the importance of the rank and file. Replacements may be plentiful, but a star employee in any role is a priceless asset. If these support roles are ignored, then the top-down approach only extends so far as mid-level managers. These clueless leaders have failed to realize that the position Carla holds gives her a great deal of influence in the branding of the company. In theory, Carla should be considered one of the organization's most important employees and should be compensated accordingly. Here we speak of compensation in terms of not only her paycheck, but also the respect she receives, acknowledgement for a job well done, and time and resources at the company's disposal allocated to ensure her top-notch performance.

The Management needs to take training these employees as a very serious matter. From this perspective, the collective front-line and administrative staff needs to be treated in a sense as being just as important as to the role played by the company's CEO. Proper coaching and delivery of performance incentives need to be given to all the "Carlas" in companies because of the critical nature of their contribution. If Carla is summarily dismissed as being unimportant to the company's success, what motivation does she have toward contributing the highest level of service of which she is capable?

The situation above is a classic example of how poor leaders incorrectly determine which employees are more important than others are; or rather, which employees should require the bulk of their attention. The Top Manager on the other hand understands how developmental directives should prioritize issues across the workforce, not just amongst "key" personnel. Each employee plays a crucial role in the leading the company along its path to success.

1.11. WATCH YOUR FOUR ELEPHANTS:
Any herd can trample you to your death.

Unskilled managers can often recognize problems with their workforce, but feel helpless as to how to improve things. What should I do to boost morale? How do I get people to take their job seriously? How do I prevent the counterproductive side effects of office politics? How do I get the most out of my employees? These questions and many more go unanswered. These managers find the only solution to the problem is to sweep it under the rug. To just "deal with it". They've acknowledged the existence of a problem, but start to consider some of these behavioral aspects of employees as unavoidable. Like the "elephant in the room".

So what about *your* elephants? Let's talk about four of them; the basic breakdown of the "elephants" you're most likely to encounter within your organization. Most organizations are comprised of employees who could be classified according to the following four categories: Under-Performers, Par-Performers, Over-Performers, and Problem-Performers. Every leader of course wishes to have only Over-Performers. Unless your company is comprised of prodigies and masterminds, this is going to be quite unlikely. You would need a limitless budget, massive amounts of time and training, and the type of patience that is normally reserved for people like the Dalai Lama. Your goal should be to get as close as you can though. You want to nurture everyone's strengths, and play down their weaknesses. In consideration, a systematic approach must be developed to manage effectively these four types of employees.

1.11.1. THE UNDER-PERFORMERS:
The Bart Simpsons are NOT role models.

One of the longest running syndications on network television can offer up a few great lessons for the Top Manager. Perhaps you remember how different the hit television show The Simpsons was back in the early 1990's. The notoriously mischievous Bart Simpson's claim to fame back then was being an "underachiever and proud of it." However, this is not a prevalent theme in the show after over twenty years on the air. After a while, the show began to receive a lot of criticism and notoriety for allegedly encouraging children who watch the show to misbehave. The show's producers ultimately realized that promoting this attitude was in effect, bad for business. As a Top Manager, you need to be able to recognize and reengineer your workforce to get rid of the type of old "Bart Simpson" habits that are bad for business.

If you have underachievers in your organization, you need to take action right away. A disdain for authority and an overall sense of apathy toward work are contagious. It can quickly spread to other employees. If certain employees are underperforming over a consistent period, the Top Manager has only two options. The first one is to realign their job duties to match ability with responsibility. If they are still underperforming, then the only choice left is to terminate them.

Again, in this tough economic environment, businesses cannot afford to keep underachieving workers on staff because it will lead to inefficiency in the company as a whole. While the company has a responsibility to contribute toward the development of an employee, this only goes so far. Let's leave the charity to the soup kitchens and not for profit agencies. The Top Manager must be emotionally tough enough to make these types of decisions because ultimately the survival of the company is at stake.

1.11.2. THE PAR-PERFORMERS:
The Peter Gibbons do not like challenges.

Popular culture is full of examples that portray office work as mundane, repetitive, tedious, and unfulfilling. Countless television shows and movies help office workers live out their fantasies of kicking down the cubicle wall, and leaving the life of the "corporate drone" behind. Think about the premise behind movies like Wanted, Fight Club, The Secret of My Success, or the old classic Nine to Five. If you are a longtime corporate employee, chances are you have also seen the movie, Office Space. Do you remember Ron Livingston's character, Peter Gibbons? When he had a life-altering epiphany about his role in the workplace, he concluded that hustle and work hard were not worth the effort. His performance was not rewarded. His contributions were not truly acknowledged, and the company's reliance on an overly bureaucratic culture meant the most attention he got was in the form of reprimand for deviating from meaningless protocols.

Peter got so sick of being called out by "seven different bosses" for a mistake on his TPS report cover pages that he began to feel the company was more concerned about compliance on the forms and memos than his actual ability to get the job done. Peter began losing interest in his job and approached tasks with a very cavalier attitude, much to the dismay and concern of his colleagues. When the company was being analyzed by efficiency consultants, whose job was to determine which employees need to be let go, Peter's profound new approach toward his job was summed up in the timeless quote, "that will only make someone work just hard enough not to get fired." Peter had realized the secret behind what motivates the "Par-Employees".

Most people in an organization are Par-Employees. They will usually perform according to their job duties and will do nothing more. Most often, they view the reward structure as having offered no incentives for them to go above and beyond. Sometimes this is the result of laziness. Other times, employees may even believe that getting attention can put them in a precarious position down the line. Instead, they want to come to work, do the minimum amount of work acceptable, collect a paycheck, and go home.

The potential issue with Par-Performers is when they become complacent and get defensive if more is added onto their workload. As a Top Manager, you must always be conscious to keep this large group in check and even more importantly, to never let them become Under-Performers. The Top Manager knows to align goals and offer incentives for these individuals to perform top-notch work. Give them a reason not to be a "Peter Gibbons".

There are two very important strategies a Top Manager can activate to avoid the manifestation of Par-Performance habits. First, it is imperative that you create a work environment that values and rewards effort and achievement. Merit based advancement is the only form of promotion that is valid or meaningful. To accomplish this, be sure employees are recognized for going above and beyond. This need not always be accompanied by a raise or promotion in responsibility; sometimes a word of recognition for a job well done should suffice.

Secondly, you need to do is instill the mindset amongst your employees that par-performance is just another form of underachieving. Most workers in this category are likely capable of much more than the status quo. Once employees begin to work at their full capacity, they will feel a greater sense of pride and ownership in their work. By creating an environment that is conducive to achievement and offering incentives for hard work, you will reduce par-performers on a consistent basis.

1.11.3. THE OVER-PERFORMERS:
The Benedict Arnolds need a special treatment.

This "elephant" is probably the most dangerous of the four. Think of the phrase "idle hands are the devil's workshop."

This principle is applicable here; let's explain why...

Benedict Arnold was a general during the American Revolutionary War. As a true American Patriot, Arnold loved his country and fought hard to prevent British Occupation. He was an excellent tactician and won many battles against British forces.

After numerous acts of bravery and going above the call of duty, Arnold was unexpectedly charged with treason. His opponents in Congress and in the Military claimed he was corrupt and was plotting against American Forces.

The investigations that pursued found that he was not only a true patriot but he also spent his own money on the war effort. Angry and bitter, Arnold decided to join British forces in 1779.

For various reasons, a few in an organization will always outperform all others. This was the case with Benedict Arnold as described in the early parts of his military career. The Top Manager must quickly identify these top performers early on because they need to be managed differently. It is critical that their success be nurtured and encouraged. The first task is to create a solid incentive system to reward their achievements. Second, you should seek to continually increase their level of responsibility because Over-Performers thrive in a challenging environment. If you misdiagnose or mismanage this group, they will leave your company to join a competitor, or worse yet, perhaps lose motivation, and begin to act in opposition to the company's best interest. The smartest most dedicated employees can also inadvertently become some of its most effective saboteurs.

Due to the nature of individuals in this category, the odds are high that they will not be with your organization for the long haul. Eventually they will outgrow most of the roles you will be able to offer them. They may even come to set their sights on your role. In fact, this is the number one reason why over-performers are mismanaged in most organizations; their supervisors are threatened and seek to hold them down.

You, as a Top Manager on the other hand, will strive to get whatever fantastic work out of the Over-Performer that you can. You will give them more and more responsibilities. Unless you are somehow able to give this individual a top position with the company, rest assured they will at some point notify you of bigger and better things. Shake this persons hand, congratulate them, and write them a glowing letter of recommendation. "It's been an honor working with you, Mr. Arnold."

1.11.4. THE PROBLEM-PERFORMERS:
The Achilles shouldn't impose their will.

According to Greek mythology, Achilles was the greatest warrior the world has ever seen. His command of the sword and battle tactics was the best. He was deemed a demigod and feared no human. He was undoubtedly the most valuable asset to the Greek army especially during the Trojan War.

In 2004, Wolfgang Petersen directed this Epic film, *TROY* in which Achilles was the main character. Similar to the legend, this blockbuster portrayed Achilles as a very skilled fighter who has been waiting his entire life to take part in the greatest battle "where legends will be made". Whoever came out victorious will have his name engraved forever as the greatest warrior. This movie went to length to emphasize also that Achilles was selfish and only interested about his "brand". He reluctantly sailed alongside the Greek Army not for country but for personal recognition. Achilles was also insubordinate, wouldn't follow the chain of command, and promised his King to have "his head on a spike before the war ends".

Problem-performers are those who, by their very nature, constantly disrupt the smooth operation of an organization. They either are engaged in constant bickering with others or are very difficult to talk to and reason with. Always itching for a fight, ready to rebel against authority, and by extension of a combative disposition, spell major trouble for the overall morale in the workplace.

Worse yet, the Problem-Performers' negative disposition is contagious. It can easily spread to other members of your team. Think about it; if the Problem-Performers' co-workers can't stand their attitude. If, on the other hand, they sympathize with the grievances of the Problem-Performers, it creates more problems. Through their antics, the Problem-Performers are severely disruptive to the work process. Consequently, they will create an unpleasant environment by which the productivity of everyone is affected. They are literally POISON to your work environment.

As a Top Manager, you simply cannot allow it. Even if your Problem-Performers are also Over-Performers like Achilles, they should not be allowed to impose their personal shortcomings on everyone around them. Typically, this condition is terminal; there is no cure. Cut out the cancer. More often than not, they must be terminated once discovered. Otherwise, it's like cutting down weeds; unless you pull them out at the root, they'll just grow back. Remember, the best leaders have to make the tough decisions and sometimes that means to part ways with even a valuable asset. You may lose a battle without your greatest warrior but by keeping them around, you may never win a war.

1.12. PLAN FOR THE WORST; EXPECT THE WORST:

Always be prepared even if the sky begins to fall.

Contingency plans are like gold. Gold that you hope you never need to use. It's why you wear your seatbelt. It's why boats should all be stocked with life preservers. It's also why every business should be locked and loaded with a bona fide disaster plan. The Top Manager understands this crucial concept: In business, you should learn to not only be prepared for, but also to expect the worst of situations. Let's face it; even the most successful companies will come up against troubling situations at times. At some point in your career, it is likely, if not certain, that you will be faced with the task of overcoming a problem of seemingly insurmountable odds. Therefore, you should brace yourself, and seriously begin considering answers to the question, "what's the worst that could happen?" This is the only way you will be ready to meet the challenge when the unthinkable does in fact happen. In doing so, you will be prepared to take action while others are hiding under their desks.

Why? Because you've already thought of solutions, what others considered unthinkable. This goes beyond the conventional platitudes of corporate "contingency" planning. These never seem to be pessimistic enough to prepare you truly for disaster. You have to imagine that the ground is going to open up and swallow your company into a pit of fire. You have to figure out what you would do if a band of machine gun toting commandos stormed through every window in the office—And everything in between. Only then, can you consider yourself truly ready. If you prepare for the worst and nothing terrible happens, consider it a "bonus".

This mindset should be your guideline when planning. Every single one of your plans should have a back-up plan with a back-up plan. For example, if the projected outlook of your business cycle for the upcoming year shows a profit, do not break out the champagne glasses and start planning your trip to Aruba. The Top Manager never rests on high expectations. Instead, you should be cautious of success, meet its arrival with trepidation, and always be developing a new plan of action. Your plan still needs to address the possibility of a catastrophic net loss, even if a comprehensive projection demonstrates otherwise.

You never know what lawsuit or disruptive technology or new development in consumer trends can threaten the very foundation of your business. As a bonus, people at every level of the company will view the prepared leader as an unwavering beacon of hope and support during a period of crisis. This goes for the Top Manager's manager as well. The Big Bosses will recognize your immense aptitude at dealing with calamity. While everyone else is frantic, this Top Manager remains calm. The planning process was set in motion long before the problem took root. If you are prepared, you already designed an easily actionable solution to resolve any particular catastrophe. In contrast, the weaker leader approaches work via the following conclusion: "If you do everything right, you will enjoy positive outcomes and positive results."

This manager is left in the reactionary position. When something "unpredicted" happens, they become helpless. In this context, let's abandon the notion of "unpredicted". You should always predict that something bad will happen. Over a long enough period, it will inevitably happen. Consider it as a mathematical certainty like one plus one will always be equal to two. Basking in the sunlight of continuing and expected success leaves you vulnerable. This should have been the cue to prepare for the storm. A manager who is unprepared for the worst invites disaster by default. Not having an ironclad, rock-solid contingency plan only encourages the organization to be characterized by chaos and uncertainty when the sky begins to fall.

The Big Question:

"HOW DO I PREPARE FOR THE WORSE?"

What strategy should you employ when planning for the worst of situations? It revolves around the concept of the early decision-making process.

First, ask yourself the following question: What is a good decision? Most of the weaker leaders will answer that a good decision will result in a positive outcome. Others will claim that a good decision has taken into consideration the right amount of diligence and caution in its conception. They are mistaken. In fact, most leaders cannot answer this question correctly.

THE CORRECT ANSWER:

A good decision is a decision that has been made already. Imagine the prospect of managing a business and making all the necessary decisions on January 1st. These decisions will cover the period from New Year's Day all the way through the close of business the following New Year's Eve. Wouldn't you be less anxious about upcoming contingencies?

Insight: The Top Managers do not make decisions to situations as they come along, but rather have formulated the proper response long before they have to implement the plan. It's simply a matter of putting these plans into action. In essence, they do not like to be faced with situations and issues they do not already have the answers for. These leaders know that in business, one of the most dangerous propositions is to make important decisions under distress when emotions and thinking prowess are not optimal. They will have a decision for the best possible scenario, the not-so likely outcome, and most importantly for the least desirable and most unthinkable of situations. With this approach, their goal of ensuring continuity as a successful going concern in the short, medium, and long term is always within their grasp. The Top Manager has already prioritized his yearly to-do list while the weaker ones are chitchatting about the amazing fireworks during the New Year's celebration in Times Square.

The Top Manager will already have the following questions:

- Under what circumstances are lay-offs necessary
- The plan of action to deal with 90% loss in revenue
- The steps to take if a key employee passes away
- The specific plan of action to take if the competition acquires a significant portion of the market
- The criteria and market condition for the company to engage in price-wars
- The direction of the company in the case of severe economic recession or depression

Weaker leaders will haphazardly attempt to answer most of these questions as they come about. Important decisions should never be made during a moment of crisis. Long before problems arise, the Top Manager has considered each possible outcome, and he has done so when the mind is calm, collected, and capacity for critical decision-making remains uncompromised by impending perils. **Planning for the worst is in essence planning for the best.** The best being the answer to any situation as undesirable as it may be.

1.13. EXCEL AT EXCELLENCE:

Mediocrity is weakness.

In basic terms, successful companies that enjoy steady financial growth are those in which the leader instills a sense of excellence on a daily basis. From the business consulting school of thought, companies who struggle to meet projections and inadequately actualize visions are normally those plagued by employee complacency and its accompanying inefficiencies.

This concept of excellence does not suggest the creation of a high stress environment in which everyone in the organization is on the brink of blowing a gasket. It means building a sense of urgency and encouraging pride in accomplishment. Flawlessness is the expectation in every task to be completed. The leader who demands excellence throughout the organization compels all employees to take on THIS special and unique state of mind.

Essentially, employees do not have tomorrow, next month or next year to become outstanding in their job duties. They have today and today only to get up to speed. This concept should extend to the role of Top Manager as well; the rationale being that it is the Top Manager's duty to get the most out of employees. This is only truly accomplished by becoming a strong and admirable leader that each employee is proud to follow. For this system to function properly, each member of the value chain must be held accountable. A good manager realizes that he or she must lead by example. The struggling manager must always stand behind the employees, looking over their shoulder, nitpicking, criticizing mundane details, having to "push" employees where he feels they need to go. The Top Manager leads from the front, while employees follow willingly.

Mediocrity is never acceptable. The "genius way" is the only standard. Accordingly, the Top Manager will make it a daily commitment to find a better system to execute regular business activities. Furthermore, this leader understands that markets change on a daily basis and as a result, businesses must adapt accordingly. For good reasons, the prospect of staying ahead of the competition relies solely on the ability of a leader to create a winning platform. This needs to be a platform that ensures the organization is always one-step ahead of the competition.

1.14. DELEGATE WITHOUT FEAR:
With efficient Systems & Controls, Courage follows.

KNOW YOUR ROLE:

Many managers lack a fundamental understanding of the extensive demands required to perform their duties adequately.

Example:

Consider for a moment the mechanic who has worked in automotive shops throughout a career spanning many years. At one point, he manages to save enough money to open his own car repair business. Now, he is the boss. No more supervisors to look over his shoulder. Without a deliberate thought process, this lifelong mechanic might fail to properly transition into his role of Manager—which holds important duties beyond those of just a mechanic. He attempts to cling to the dual role of managing the operational aspects of the business while also supervising and participating in the daily repairs. In his near-sighted assessment, fixing cars is the most important task in the shop because it is the major source of income, without which his business would not survive.

He may feel that because he is the most capable mechanic in the shop, it makes absolute sense for him to conduct and oversee the majority of the repairs. After all, this ensures that jobs are completed in a timely fashion and free of costly blunders ...

Sounds reasonable, right?

Of course not; his managerial role will remain conspicuously undermanned, or worse yet practically vacant. The reality will wind up being that a disproportionate amount of his time is spent putting out fires. The likelihood of his business surviving long-term is slim. Businesses such as these never even had a chance.

THE BOTTOM LINE:

The responsibilities of a leader are fixed, regardless of how important some tasks may appear.

This example describes how scary it is for weaker leaders to delegate important tasks to their team. This is often accompanied by the mistaken belief that the act constitutes surrendering a part of their authority. They may feel anxious about the employee's ability to perform up to par. They may even be concerned that, given the opportunity to shine, an employee will outperform the manager. This manager is often a very capable individual who assumes there is no way this employee will be able to do the job as well as him. This last assumption is often correct. The person to whom an important task is delegated is usually not as skilled in his/her performance as the delegator is.

The erroneous part of this assumption is that the skill differential between the "delegator" and "delegate" really matters. Think of it from the perspective of the Law of Diminishing Marginal Returns. The Top Manager only has so much time in a day. The Top Manager also realizes, due to the pressing demands on this precious and limited resource, that there is no possible way to meet all of these challenges alone.

This requires delegating tasks, some of which are often key initiatives and the performance of critical functions. While hiring someone as capable as him would be terribly cost ineffective, surely the Top Manager can find someone adequately adept at the performance of a given task. With this function delegated to an able-bodied participant, the Top Manager is freed up to focus on big picture issues, the execution of which will drive the generation of new revenue making scenarios. You can see why this arrangement is optimal, as opposed to the Top Manager having taken the shortsighted approach to completing the would-be delegated task perfectly. Diminishing Marginal Returns are at play once again.

You want things on automatic. However, setting things up to run in the Top Manager's absence is no easy task in and of itself. To accomplish this structure, the Top Manager needs to ensure that everyone understands their role, what is expected, and that each delegate is capable of expert execution of their assigned tasks. The Top Manager will utilize the two most important tools in business: Systems and Controls. We will cover extensively systems and controls in Section 3, but for now, how about an appetizer?

Let's illustrate this concept using the "car" as an example. Cars are full of moving parts. These parts that need to work together flawlessly in order to keep the system running. The car is a system that gets us from one point to another. In order to accomplish this goal safely and properly, the car requires a distinct set of systems and controls.

Systems are simply the engine of an organization. For example, let us consider the vehicle owned by a hapless and unsuspecting individual named Sam. Sam couldn't put together a plan of action to save his life. His bills are normally past due, his performance at work is subpar, his grace with social interactions and romance is virtually nonexistent, and elements of his appearance would lead one to conclude his personal hygiene leaves not much to be desired. However, Sam is able to drive his automobile from one place to another. The car is one of the most dynamic and earth-shattering inventions the world has ever seen. An extremely complex and fascinating collection of interactive devices all working as one for a common goal. Sam couldn't explain one thing about this invention, save the fact that he realizes it gets him from place to place.

Sam's vehicle has an engine with numerous parts interconnected for the efficient operation of his vehicle. The brake system is responsible for slowing the car down or completely stopping it if necessary. The cooling system is responsible for providing enough aeration so that his vehicle will not overheat. The transmission system is responsible for providing enough power for his car to pick up speed and ride for long distances. The gas pump is responsible for providing the right amount energy so that his vehicle stays running. Those above are just some of the systems that comprise Sam's vehicle.

Every time Sam starts his car, hundreds of procedures take effect to make his engine operate. The most wonderful reality about Sam's vehicle is that he never has to dictate to his engine how to execute its regular functions. The engine knows what procedures to follow and what actions to commence the moment Sam turns the key in the ignition. This excellent partnership is possible because Sam's car manufacturer implemented the engine systems long before it arrived in Sam's parking lot. Because of the pre-constructed systems in Sam's car, he only has to provide it with regular maintenance so he can operate it for years to come. Additionally, someone else besides Sam can drive the vehicle and it will perform the same exact way. The perpetually ill-fated and unfortunate Sam is able to accomplish what would have been miracles a mere century ago, just by making sure he gets his car to the shop for routine maintenance.

Top Managers will strive to build their organizations like car engines so even the "Sams" of the world are able to take the reins if needs be. Their organizations will be built piece by piece and all of the necessary mechanisms will be in place long before any employee is required to perform a task. For good reasons, they put their employees in a frame in which they cannot change the predetermined course or debate over the next plan of action. Just like cars, business systems represent the sets of structures that must take effect in coordination with predetermined controls to make an organization run efficiently. If true systems and controls are in place in an organization, then a leader will be able to delegate full authority to anyone with the confidence that operational activities will be executed at a maximum level of excellence.

However, one should be careful not to mistake systems as synonymous with standard procedures. In reality, standard procedures are the manuals that one will use to operate the systems. Most organizations only have standard procedures. Without systems, standard procedures are meaningless because they amount to a multitude of rules with a limited chance of implementation. Consequently, these organizations always face efficiency and consistency issues. Their major problem lies not in their ability to write up many rules and regulations but their inability to construct a business model that is operational all year long and in every type of business activity.

1.15. REACH FOR THE MOON:

Everything else is as risky as planning for a rocket launch.

Rome wasn't built in a day, right? Success takes time. You have to put your time in. We are taught not to shoot for the moon on our first rocket launch. Progress is made one grain of sand at a time. River sediment takes thousands and thousands of years to form a delta. It builds up through the continual acceleration of tiny sediment particles deposited at the mouth of the river. Year after year. One layer on top of another. Gradually, something amazing takes shape.

Eventually these accumulate into a large landmass with fertile soil, rich in nutrients, replete with organic matter and ideal for new growth—New Beginnings. Your efforts and ideas should be the same way. Hard work yields the same results. Piece by piece, you construct the foundation of your success. Each new idea or day of work is another grain of sand to build your own river delta; a fertile backdrop for your long-term aspirations. However, are you accumulating the right ideas and concepts?

With these principles in mind, we may go to college. Look for a steady job with benefits and "stability". We punch the clock. Pay into our 401k. Try to avoid taking too many risks. We have aspirations of slowly but surely climbing the career ladder. After all, it's practical. Because of this near-sighted notion, many people are dissuaded from bold and decisive action for the sake of practicality.

> *"If I risk everything, I won't have the financial safety net I need to get by."*
>
> *"I have bills to pay, how can I take that kind of risk?"*
>
> *"What if I fail, then I'll be left with nothing"*

True statements. Anyone who argues the contrary would be ignoring blatantly obvious facts. However, these only tell one side of the story. Ask yourself, **what if ...**

"... The bottom dropped out on the economy?"

"... The business model is currently useless since everyone is doing the same exact thing?"

"... I got fired, or downsized, or my company went out of business?"

In the late 2000s, the United States and world economies were facing an uncertain future. Unemployment had reached new heights with no promise of abatement in the short term. The number of people who were "underemployed" was yet another frighteningly indeterminable figure. This is a time where the traditional practicality of higher education became less and less iron clad.

According to the 2010 Census, the number of janitors with college degrees rose 87% in the ten years prior. This figure is just a sliver of the tens of thousands of newly minted college graduates who are unable to find work in their intended field. The even larger group of overeducated workers doesn't count those who toiled in their vocation for years; only to be shown the door when business went bad. These individuals chose college and a career as an investment. Some of them worked hard to pay for it themselves, some received tuition money from family members, and many others decided to leverage this "investment" with student loan debt. How many young people are scrambling now to avoid defaulting on their student loans? How many seasoned career professionals and would-be retirees have lost their pension or the bulk of their 401k with stock market crashes?

One cannot help but wonder whether the "safe" route is still a good choice. Was it truly practical to rely on convention? Pursuing the traditional norms sounds as though it is becoming just as risky as your average entrepreneurial startup. Is it still truly NOT practical to swing for the fences? To want to put your footprints in the Sea of Tranquility for future generations to admire with wonder? You can't get there without taking a shot. You can probably start and fail at a business venture for a lot less money than it would cost to go to college. In addition, you'd be no worse off than the college educated waiter on line cook. So why not shoot for the moon?

Maybe your first rocket launch doesn't even get off the ground. Maybe it blows up in your face. At least you aimed high. And if you missed your mark, you closely and honestly evaluate your failures. Become intimately familiar with your missteps. Then, take every possible lesson along with you into your next attempt. If you didn't make it to your target, there's no doubt you discovered a few ways NOT to do something. Instead of being content launching weather balloons to survey the atmosphere, you need to be considering bigger opportunities. Is there a way you can break the bonds of gravity to explore the moon?

This is an important concept for the Top Manager's mindset. Each day we are confronted with the pressure to remain within the boundaries prescribed by tradition. As managers and leaders, we are also dissuaded from bold and decisive actions. We are encouraged not to take calculated risks. The Top Manager however must recognize that a pattern of inaction and status quo complacency are equally as risky. The Top Manager must be prepared to make moves that make a difference—*TO SHOOT FOR THE MOON.*

SECTION II -
MASTER THE
BUSINESS
ANALYSIS:

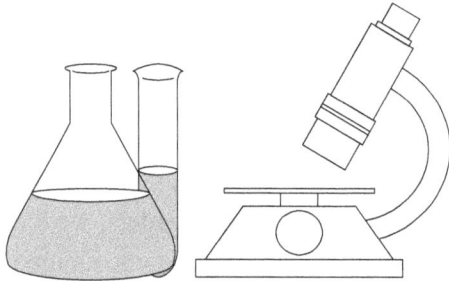

Why is it that the medical profession remains one of the fastest growing industries on the planet? Despite profound advancements in the capabilities of medicine and health over the past century, people still get sick. People still die. People still have the need to seek the advice of a doctor. Now we're keeping people alive longer than ever before. Some medical health scientists project that as of the turn of the millennium, the first humans to live past 150 years of age have already been born. Much of this is estimated to be a byproduct of the leaps and bounds that have been made in medical care technology and techniques. People young and old alike will always have the need for qualified and competent emergency room nurses, staff, and personnel.

One major change in the application of modern medicine however is present in the paradigm shift toward preventative care. In our quest for longevity and health, perfectly healthy people seek the advice of medical professionals. People look to the experts for guidance as to living a healthy lifestyle, and best practices in preventing debilitating health issues. So why should we treat the health of a business any different?

For many organizations, it's difficult for their leadership to take a step back to conduct an honest assessment and accurately identify the health problems that exist within the company. With this approach, problem-solving remains a constant headache for the weaker managers; and blindly taking Aspirin doesn't always make it go away. For the less adroit managers, problems are often evident once symptoms begin to show, but figuring out where they start remains a mystery. Addressing issues in this fashion is akin to putting a Band-Aid on a gunshot wound. On the other hand, being able to find the root cause of a given operational illness allows the Top Manager to properly assess a problem and determine the proper course of treatment for its eradication.

What the Top Manager knows and others have yet to figure out is that uncovering the cause of the troubling symptoms is best accomplished through the implementation of a systematic analysis process for the critical areas of the organization. The doctor does the same thing when you come in to complain of recurring symptoms or chronic pains. Your physician will begin by asking you basic questions. Your responses will give him an idea as to what investigative path to pursue and will shape each following question. Finally, the doctor will be able to offer a preliminary diagnosis and recommend a course of action to treat the problem. In this same fashion, the Top Manager is able to uncover and treat sources of problems in a business, sometimes even before symptoms begin to manifest.

We will classify this same fact-finding practice in the corporate world as the "Business Analysis". In all respects, the business analysis performs thorough "X-Ray" of the organization's operational activities. Every major functional issue and any symptom of inefficiency will be brought to the surface once this assessment is complete. Now, the Top Manager is faced only with the task of counteracting a clearly defined problem. The methods one would take to treat the discovered problems come with a bit more certainty, and the *business health* is not left to fate. Essentially, the task of problem solving becomes easier, faster, and more absolute.

THE BASICS OF A GOOD BUSINESS ANALYSIS:

In this section, we're going to cover a variety of topics as pertaining to the execution of a thorough and proper business analysis. This is essentially a detailed overview of a business' financial and operational health.

You will definitely realize the ease in solving typical business problems once you master the following business analysis tools:

1. Comparative Cost Analysis
2. Z-Score Analysis
3. Break-Even Analysis
4. Management Tools & Capabilities Analysis
5. Organizational Structure Analysis
6. Standard Procedures Analysis
7. Employees' Performance Analysis
8. Goals & Objectives Analysis
9. Marketing & Promotional Strategy Analysis
10. Operational Systems & Controls Analysis
11. Financial Structure Analysis
12. Entity Structure & Tax Strategy Analysis

2.1. COMPARATIVE COST ANALYSIS (CCA):
Spotlighting inefficiencies is easier with a simple model.

The Comparative Cost Analysis (CCA) may initially sound scary. In reality, it is one of the easiest business concepts to absorb and apply. On the importance scale, the CCA is by far one of the most beneficial tools in a business analysis. Undoubtedly, if more managers recognized its commanding utility, then more businesses would enjoy the luxury of consistent profitability. As its name depicts, the CCA performs a side-by-side examination of the financial efficiency of an organization through its cost structures. In other words, the CCA determines if overspending has occurred.

First, let's outline the basic principles of the CCA.

2.1.1. EXPENSES VS. INVESTMENTS:
Every dime spent in a business is an investment.

The CCA model treats every EXPENSE in an organization as an INVESTMENT. For example, a regular company will view office supplies like paper and pencils as expenses.

Are they really? Let's find out!

Example:

COMPANY SUPERTOP writes a proposal to client Y to bid for a project, which will generate $100,000 in revenues. What will COMPANY SUPERTOP do?

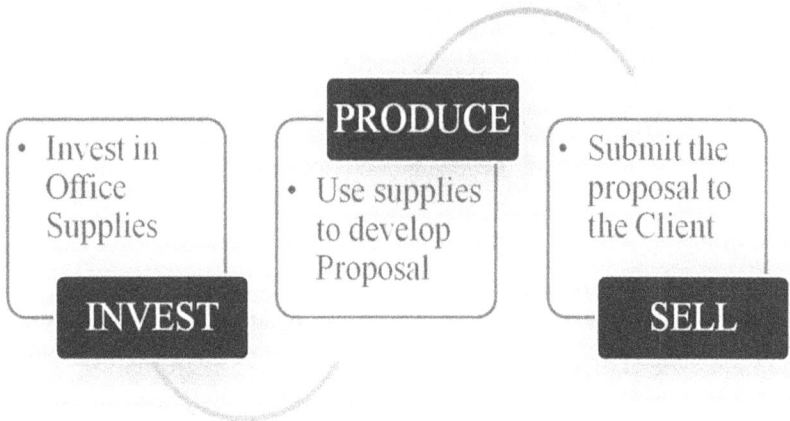

INVEST	PRODUCE	SELL
• Invest in Office Supplies	• Use supplies to develop Proposal	• Submit the proposal to the Client

THE POINT ...

to get the client to select Company ABC for the Project

Even though other resources like human capital were part of the proposal-writing process, the paper was still an integral part in the submittal of the bid. Therefore, we can conclude that office supplies are indeed investments.

2.1.2. RETURN ON INVESTMENT (ROI):

Business Success is simply about the bottom line.

Since we are discussing investments, then ROIs must follow. ROIs are simply what you receive in return when investing in something. While a ROI is calculated a number of ways, each taking into account different expenditure levels or factors, the CCA takes a unique look in regards to applying the concept toward items like office supplies and overhead. Take a look...

Example:

Assume in 2006, COMPANY SUPERTOP spent (invested) $10,000 in office supplies and generated $100,000 in revenue.

Question:

What is the ROI for investing $10,000 in office supplies?

Answer:

FORMULA: REVENUE ÷ INVESTMENT

Therefore:

$100,000 (Revenue) ÷ $10,000 (Investment in Office Supplies) = **$10 = ROI**

$10 means: For every $1 spent in office supplies in 2006, COMPANY SUPERTOP received $10 in return.

Strategy:

Any investment incurred in an organization should be directly associated to revenue to calculate the subsequent return.

The purpose here is not to suggest that office supplies in fact constitute an actual investment with a 1,000% return. More importantly, the purpose of this illustrative exercise is to emphasize the importance of frequently overlooked costs. Businesses take great pains in measuring all types of capital expenditures. From an analytic standpoint, however, it all too often seems that overhead dollars are thrown into a black hole.

2.1.3. THE FOUR PERIODS MINIMUM:
Analyzing a trend will reveal a pattern.

The CCA model requires at least four periods to evaluate general cost trends effectively and to determine the highest return. These periods can be 4 years, 4 quarters, 4 months, or even 4 days. It simply depends on the nature of the business cycle and the availability information.

Now that you understand the basic premises of the CCA, let's work out an example.

Let's assume the following about COMPANY SUPERTOP:

Year	2006	2007	2008	2009
Revenue	$100,000	$91,000	$128,000	$144,000
Office Supplies	$10,000	$7,000	$16,000	$12,000

Return On Investment:

Year	2006	2007	2008	2009
Revenue	$100,000	$91,000	$128,000	$144,000
Office Supplies	$10,000	$7,000	$16,000	$12,000
ROI	$10	$13	$8	$12

As you can tell in this example, the revenue is irrelevant. In fact, the year with the highest revenue did not produce the highest ROI. As you can tell, he highest ROI occurred when revenue was at its lowest in the 4 years shown above.

IT IS NOT ALL ABOUT REVENUES...
IT'S ALL ABOUT RETURNS.

After conducting the ROI, we are able to establish the $13 return (achieved in 2007) as our standard moving forward.

Comparative Cost Analysis:

The next step in our basic CCA exercise is to apply the BEST ROI calculated above to every year in the period. This model operates on the premise that once a high standard is achieved, the organization is then required to perform at the same level or above. At its core, this requirement is the guiding light; it prevents the situation wherein a substandard return is ever acceptable. In simple words, if you have done something well, then you are expected to repeat it. After all, you have already proven your ability to do it. If the ROI of $13 is not achieved every year prior and every year thereafter, we must conclude that overspending has occurred.

IDEAL COST:

IDEAL COST = SALES ÷ NEWEST STANDARD ROI

This is the amount that should have been spent had the best ROI been achieved in any other year in the four period model. To calculate the Ideal Cost, divide each year's revenue by the highest standard as shown next:

Year	2006	2007	2008	2009
Sales	$100,000	$91,000	$128,000	$144,000
Newest Standard ROI	$13	$13	$13	$13
IDEAL COST	**$7,692**	**$7,000**	**$9,846**	**$11,077**

THREE POINTS TO CONSIDER:

1. The Ideal Cost represents the sum COMPANY SUPERTOP should have spent on office supplies if the best ROI ($13) is applied
2. The Ideal Cost in 2007 for office supplies is equal to the current cost as it is the year when the highest standard was achieved
3. This best ROI was applied retroactively, as this model also assumes that the best ROI could have been attained at any given time during the 4 periods

USE THIS PROVEN
MODEL AND YOU WILL
ENGINEER EFFICIENCY.

IN THE LONG-TERM, YOU
WILL SECURE YOUR

SAFETY NET.

Excess Cost:

To get the excess cost, subtract the Ideal Cost from the Current Cost.

EXCESS COST = CURRENT COST — OPTIMAL COST

	Current Cost	—	Optimal Cost	=	Excess Cost
2006	$10,000	—	$7,692	=	$2,308
2007	$7,000	—	$7,000	=	$0
2008	$16,000	—	$9,846	=	$6,154
2009	$12,000	—	$11,077	=	$923
			Total		**$9,385**

Based on this CCA, we can conclude that COMPANY SUPERTOP has overspent $9,385 in office supplies from 2006 to 2009. Accordingly, the profit of COMPANY SUPERTOP was reduced by $9,385 from 2006 to 2009.

Moving Forward:

Now that you understand the CCA process, test your knowledge using a complete Profit and Loss (P&L) statement. **(Go to Appendix 1).**

2.2. Z-SCORE ANALYSIS:

Knowing the Credit Score of a company is imperative.

2.2.1. THE IMPORTANCE:

A forgotten hero needs to be remembered once a while.

The Z-Score calculation is a crucial part of any business analysis. It sheds light on the solvency and the financial strength of a company. In simple terms, the higher the Z-Score, the higher the chances for long-term sustainability. Furthermore, a company with a healthy Z-Score will have less trouble securing funds from financial institutions and venture capitalists. In fact, the Z-Score represents the "Credit Score" of a business.

2.2.2. THE HISTORY:

The main champion for the Z-Score analysis is Professor Edward Altman. He developed this concept and formula in 1968 after concluding a study of over 60 mid-sized companies. There are countless other resources for detailed review of Z-Scores and their utility. Just to refresh or introduce the reader, however, in this section we will give a brief overview in order to demonstrate its utility.

2.2.3. THE BASICS:

To calculate the Z-Score, you will need the information from both the P&L and the Balance Sheet statements. You must be adept at reading and analyzing financial statements because they are the foundation of any financial analysis. On a side note, other Z-Score formulas exist to place more weight on the variations that constitute businesses.

Here are some:

1. Privately Held Vs. Publically Held Firm
2. Manufacturing Vs. Non-Manufacturing Firm
3. Financial Vs. Non-Financial Firm

Moving Forward:

To learn how to develop a Z-Score for a business, go to **Appendix 2.**

2.3. OPTIMUM BREAK-EVEN ANALYSIS:

Understanding your daily cost of operation should be a priority.

The Break-Even analysis is a critical component of the daily management of a business. Essentially, it establishes the minimum revenue requirement a company must reach to cover its financial obligations. The Break-Even Point is also referred to as the "Zero-Profit Point". An Optimum Break-Even point takes into account an amount required to generate an acceptable **profit**, and considers this item to be an additional **expense**. It is congruent with the old adage for personal savings that you always need to "pay yourself first". The Break-Even Point is also very versatile and can be used to support many managerial decisions. Without the Break-Even points for example, the marketing department wouldn't be able to determine effectively the minimum sales goal of a company in order to stay afloat. This is the reason why this analysis is so important.

Moving Forward:

To learn how to develop Optimum Break-Even Points for a business, go to **Appendix 3.**

2.4. MANAGEMENT TOOLS & CAPABILITIES:
Learn to separate Fact from Fiction and you may conquer the universe.

2.4.1. EXPERTISE VS. ABILITY:
Do not get stuck in semantics?

Many people are promoted to leadership positions based on their demonstrated proficiency in a specific field. We consider this as EXPERTISE. The rationale behind promoting these people is that they possess the necessary command over the subject matter to facilitate dissemination of this knowledge to the rest of a team. In essence, they knew how to "do something really well" and it was enough to convince their supervisors that they were fit to lead. It is the natural continuum for the status quo. They have put in their years of service. They showed up most days, didn't call in sick too often, and usually arrived to work on time. They kept their head down, did their work very well, stayed out of trouble, and demonstrated their loyalty to the company. They DESERVE to be promoted, right?

The assumption itself is not without some merit, but these scenarios do not always play out as anticipated. Presuming a certain level of expertise in a seasoned employee is not an error in and of itself. However, one cannot assume this same subject matter expert will transition into an effective manager of people. Leading a team is an entirely different skill set in comparison to job proficiency. Expertise in a certain field is important, but is not always transferable into leadership ability.

We will refer to this phenomenon as the "Expertise vs. Ability" dilemma. The "Ability" factor refers to the managerial prowess of a leader. At the very least, an effective manager possesses the aptitude to instill confidence within a team and develop the proper strategies to achieve the predetermined goals. The perfect scenario would be for managers to possess both the expertise and the ability. However, in many cases, they often tend to have a higher concentration in one area over the other.

This analysis seeks to find if decisions to promote managers were based on expertise, or ability or both. As the Top Manager, you must remain conscious of this reality when assigning managerial seats. Were your choices made based on expertise, or was ability the primary factor? It's not going to help the organization to have an expert who cannot lead. The employees will not receive clear direction and the quality of their work will suffer. These unable managers will not be able to lead effectively their team; their work will suffer as well. This will be the cause for much stress on both sides of the equation. And it will only make your job more difficult when you realize you have to fire, demote, dismiss, or handle the monsters you've created.

It is important to recognize the fact that many managers will use their expertise as a platform to justify their ill-advised actions. It is possible that they have mastered the art of disguising or misrepresenting their expertise as supposed ability. They may even have garnered support from coworkers who would prefer to deal with a manager they already know rather than a stranger brought in from the outside. So consider the issue closely. Examine your motives for choosing to promote a given individual. It is your responsibility to figure out where the expertise stops and where the ability begins.

An aspiring manager who possesses expertise but perhaps poor leadership skills might claim the following:

"I deserve this leadership position. I've paid my dues! I've worked in this field since the new recruits were in grade school; they stand to learn a lot from me!"

Your response should be: "I am not trying to determine if you are an expert at what you do. I want to assess your leadership abilities. I just want to find out if you are the right person for this role."

It must be clear that **leadership prowess is valued above technical expertise** when it comes to the managerial function. After all, the leader is delegating the operational tasks. This principle illustrates itself in many other aspects of life. Think, for instance, about when you pay someone to mow your lawn, clean your house, or even do your taxes. Most of these things you could probably do yourself. And that includes the taxes. However, are you an expert? Do you have the time? You delegate these things to people who specialize in these tasks, and simply through the act of ongoing repetition have gained a strong proficiency for their fast and proficient execution. Does this mean you can't spot when they've been performed improperly? Absolutely not.

This point must be clear to those wishing to attain the supervisory role, and it must be communicated to the employees over whom this manager will preside. A Manager has to possess only an acceptable mastery of the subject matter at hand. This should be sufficient to gauge performance and offer guidance. A solid Leadership Ability will enable a manager to drive the team to accomplish feats beyond everyone's expectations.

2.4.2. DECISION-MAKING PROCESS:
There is way to look into the future.

Decisions should be deliberate, unfettered, decisive, and forward thinking. They must reached through a systematic analysis of the relevant factors. The decision-making process is a distinct blend of art and science. In the fast-paced environment of the business world, not every situation will allow a decision to consider all measurable factors. On that same note, no decision-making process should ever be undertaken on a purely emotionally responsive gut-feeling basis. This analysis determines the process by which senior managers make decisions on a daily basis in your organization.

When your company faces a tough choice, you need to analyze carefully what happens. You should always begin by ascertaining the following:

- Who wants to get willingly involved when a crisis arises?
- Does a team-brainstorming session occur?
- Does a Cost-Benefit analysis occur?
- How long does it take to implement decisions?
- What and who are the obvious barriers to implementing decisions effectively?
- Are decisions centralized or departmentalized?

The answers to the questions above are critical, as no decision-making process is carried out in a controlled environment. The ultimate choice will have far-reaching consequences, whether good or bad. It is important to consider the domino effect caused by any given situation. The Top Manager always looks to see ten steps ahead. In this regard, determining the answers to the above questions is critical for the following three reasons:

It helps you understand the internal dynamics of the organization as well as who could become your valuable assets during a moment of crisis

The results of this analysis will later help you construct the best possible organizational structure

It will help you bypass the negative forces that will stall your progress and continued development

2.4.3. DICTATORS VS. SOCIALISTS:

Extremes are helpful sometimes.

For this discussion, abandon all general precepts you may have regarding political affiliations and think about what you know to be true regarding these different schools of thought. Consider the extreme ends of the scale for each type of regime. Certainly, at either end you can come up with a list of at least five fatal faults. As is the case with the political process, these societal viewpoints and modalities have applicability at the microeconomic social level as well. Extremes are unhealthy at any level. Let's extend this discussion to the characteristics of different managers.

The "Dictator." You've met this person before at some point in your career. Hopefully, it was not in gazing admiringly into the mirror. This type of manager makes demands without the possibility for input or feedback. No compromise. No vote. No deals. The "Dictator" usually retains the exclusive right to make decisions and expects everyone to obey without question or delay. Dictators can be feared managers because they project a constant imposing authority and unyielding power. Ideas from down the chain of command, even good ones, are dismissed as inferior automatically. The Dictators are often ill tempered and quick to set place on fire. These traits often accompany the domineering disposition held by the dictatorial managers.

At the opposite end of the spectrum are the "Socialists". Egalitarian process and social equality take precedence over many other important business issues. Everyone must have a say. Everyone must be on board—the business world's embodiment of groupthink. The Socialist type managers consistently involve each member of the team in obtaining a consensus as part of the decision-making process. After all, shouldn't they play a role in arriving at a decision that will affect everyone? Simply put, the Socialist managers are more likely to engage everyone in critical decision points, even when soliciting their input is counterproductive. Employees' motives may not always be aligned with the best interest of the company. Furthermore, yielding to the whims of the workforce can compromise the leader's ultimate authority, particularly when input is sought from all levels for all decisions. The Socialist managers are often the ones who try hard to be "friends" with their staff. This is a dangerous move, and will ultimately compromise their authority, and thus weakens their ability to lead effectively a team.

These two basic classifications are not limited to managers alone. They are indicative of belief systems and ideas held by individual members of your team. Each member of the organization has leanings one way or the other to a certain degree. As the Top Manager, it is your responsibility to identify which members of your staff fall into a certain category. It is important, because it has a major bearing on how certain team members will interact with their managers and with one another. Keep in mind that the existence of each type of these managers can be beneficial to the company.

The Top Manager knows which type of leadership style compels which employee to accomplish which task. It is even beneficial for an individual manager to possess traits of each. No doubt, we could engage in a longwinded discussion as to the positives and perils associated with each type of leader. The fact is: each one has his strengths in different situations. Each one also has his weaknesses. Your goal as the Top Manager is to establish the best composition and this analysis will allow you to do it.

2.4.4. TECHNICAL SKILLS:

Everything will be so much different in 100 years.

We haven't quite reached the era of flying cars, hover-boards and digital display athletic shoes like we were promised by time travel movies of the 1980's, but we're getting closer. Take a moment to consider how awe-stricken consumers were the first time they saw wireless internet in action. Now people throw a temper tantrum if a webpage takes more than a few seconds to load on their smartphones. Put this in perspective. Try to be thankful that we live in a world where the free flow of information and ingenuity allow these feats to be possible. Now take another moment to consider the future implications. Take a moment to be scared that grade-schoolers are being taught how to write software codes, while many adults have trouble synching their Outlook email.

This underscores the desperate need to have tech savvy staff members on your team. You need to evaluate their capabilities and expertise in the areas of information technology, software, database management, internet marketing and the impact these subjects will have on your organization's ability to turn a profit. Having a technologically inclined staff is imperative. Not only should you determine their exact limitations when it comes to technology but also their unspoken fears and limitations. Take them out of their comfort zone, and introduce them to new technologies that will help grow the business. Understand your own limitations as well. The knowledge acquired from this analysis will help you determine the types of training programs you will pursue for your team, your business, and yourself.

Let's say your goal is to overhaul the entire IT infrastructure of your organization. No doubt, this will spell momentary inconvenience for all, as well as a stall in productivity for the company. However, look at the long-term. By the time you need to throw out your obsolete computers to buy the new ones that are ten times faster and hundred times more powerful (aka, next week), new business systems and online platforms will almost require your whole-hearted participation to remain competitive. The change might be hard, but it's necessary. And the sooner you initiate it, the better. Be ready to be met with opposition, as people are often resistant to change. It is important to assess the ease with which you can integrate the overhaul, and be sure to broadcast this well ahead of time. Also, let people know how important it is to their own professional development. By putting your company ahead of the technological curve, you are doing a favor for everyone involved.

Your employees get a richer and more meaningful work experience. It will streamline certain elements of the company's business operations. It will provide clients and customers with a higher quality and timelier end product or service, and as the Top Manager, you will surely be viewed as visionary and forward thinking. It may even serve you well to seek input and suggestions from the employees, who will be affected by the changes. You might be surprised how much some of them know. Employees will be a good source of input when choosing how and when to implement new technological systems. They have the frontline experience that will give them unique insights as to the benefits of new technology. In other words, if you miss the mark, they may not. Above all, when communicating the message regarding an impending change to the work environment, you can counteract resistance to change by outlining the following three principles:

1. Make sure they understand the necessity to overhaul the current systems
2. Let them know you believe they can understand and use the new systems
3. Demonstrate your sincere intention to help you, them, and the company to be more competitive

2.4.5. FINANCIAL SKILLS:

Understanding numbers will enlighten your path.

You must not only speak the language, but be able to read it as well. Think of the world of financial accounting as being a foreign country. If you're on vacation, you might be able to get by with a basic knowledge of the local culture and a few memorized phrases. Nevertheless, "donde esta el baño" will only ever get you to one place. And guess what that place is full of? As a Top Manager, you have several other places you need to explore; places you need to take your organization. And you won't be able to accomplish your organization's goals unless you can speak the mother tongue of business; the language of money.

Where it goes, how it comes in, how it's recorded, and what each element of a financial statement means. You need to have a comfortable understanding of what transactions have which effects on your income statement, your balance sheet, and the bottom line, and how these aspects interact with one and other. You need to have some level of fluency in order to interface with the "natives". If you don't, they will no doubt become restless. They will see a tourist, who is an obvious mark, and will pick your pockets clean and rob you blind.

As you may suspect, finance and accounting are the motors behind the management of an organization. Financial records and projections provide crucial information as to where the organization has been and where it is going. How much cash do we have on hand? How long is it taking us to turn over our receivables? What are our liquidity measures? Will we need to take on new debt? Can we discharge old debt? What covenants does the bank impose on our operations as a condition of taking on or discharging this debt? While the CFO or your team of accountants, or your office manager, or whatever expert you have in charge of the organization's finances will likely be the one managing the day-to-day finances, as the Top Manager, you are ultimately responsible for the organization's financial performance.

This is to include an intimate knowledge of your company's fiscal health and financial position. Otherwise, you risk the prospect of letting the kid run the cash register at the candy store. Finances are inextricably tied to every element of business operations. The majority of a company's systems, controls, and strategies revolve around financial and accounting records, measures, and operations. It is very critical for the Top Manager to demonstrate a minimum level of competency in regards to finance and accounting. In many organizations for example, funds are swindled or misappropriated because those in charge misunderstand the general route of money through the computing and reporting processes. A clever accountant can lay intricate shell games to cover up a dollar's journey throughout the business cycle. A dimwitted accountant can also lose millions by accident. When these oversights become known, it's usually too late.

So how does this work in practice? Let us assume that you assessed the financial and accounting knowledge of a senior manager and concluded that this person lacked the requisite proficiency level. How he got there is a secondary concern. How and how much longer he stays there is another issue. However, your immediate priority is to scrutinize quickly a range of financial transactions to ensure you have accurate and up-to-date information in your reports. In a situation where you've determined your financial "expert" to be deficient in the execution of his duties, it is likely you will be opening up a big juicy can of worms. Even one accounting mistake can be amplified and interwoven with others as time moves forward. In addition, this is a best-case scenario. Whether unwittingly or by design, having the wrong person in charge of accounting functions creates an environment that is extremely vulnerable to fraud and error.

The American Institute of Certified Public Accountants (AICPA) acknowledges that in most cases, fraud is a crime of opportunity that is usually mitigated by employing the proper internal financial controls. Concepts such as "separation of duties", where the handling of financial process control procedures are assigned to two or more competent employees. More eyes means less chances for mistakes, and less of chances for dishonesty, as this would now require collusion. Internal controls dictate how an organization's resources are directed, monitored, and measured. Other examples of effective internal controls include "authorization of transactions", where an official process is in place to ensure the validity of individual actions. "Retention of records" in a fashion that provides useful, accurate, and timely information to management is also crucial. Without this, your business will essentially have "money amnesia".

As the Top Manager, you don't need to be a financial accounting genius or spend weeks auditing old transactions, but you do need to know enough to assess the internal control environment and be effectively able to identify and mitigate significant risks to your reporting process. This includes a thorough evaluation of your employees who serve in this capacity. With this analysis, you can confirm the type of training programs you will seek for your employees or how many pink slips you need to hand out.

2.4.6. CONNECTIONS:

Hate or love it, it pays to know people.

It pays to know people. Have you ever heard the phrase, "it's not what you know, but who you know?" Admittedly, it is a tired cliché. However, there is a lot of truth to this old axiom. Spend some time searching for a job, and you'll quickly realize how important it is to have inside connections and a strong network in your industry. Your reputation often precedes you. Whether good, bad, or indifferent, once you reach a certain level in any given line of work, people around town will likely know who you are. Even a large city like Washington D.C. or New York becomes a small community when you break it down by profession. The reason being, they've all worked with one another, changed jobs, and worked with other people with whom you worked, and changed jobs again and worked with you, and so on.

If you put a bunch of dots up on a whiteboard and started drawing lines between them like a chemical compound illustration, you would see that people in a given profession are intimately connected. Real Estate Investors know most of the other local or regional Real Estate Investors. Car dealership owners know just about every other owner of a car dealership within a 100-mile radius.

Over the course of a career, a person who has worked for three or four of the major companies in their industry will wind up working with a guy who worked with a lady she worked with at her previous job, or vice versa, or both, or whatever. The point is: it's a small world. You have to try to meet everyone who has some type of influence or power, or purchasing ability. You have to know the people who can help you. You have to know that you never know how other people can prove to be an asset at some point down the line. Build bridges, and try your best not to light them on fire. You never know when you'll need to cross that ravine again.

So it becomes apparent having some degree of networking proficiency can be an important attribute of managers. Some leaders understand the importance of being well connected and others dwell happily within their shells. In some cases, the types of connections the managers possess make the difference between getting millions of dollars in revenues and scrambling to meet the minimum sales goals.

The following are a few questions, you should ask:

- Do your senior managers understand the importance of being well connected?
- Do they regularly attend trade shows?
- Do they participate in networking events, meet-ups, etc.?
- Do they have solid contacts with the local business groups or associations?

If the answer to any of these questions is "no", it is time to start thinking about what needs to be done to change this. If you are not exhausting all avenues by which to be known, and to know everyone else that is worth knowing you are missing out. The Top Manager needs to learn how to be a "politician" in some regards.

Rest assured that your competitors are doing this. They are out there shaking hands, kissing babies, and coordinating lunch meetings all for the sake of the business. You probably should be too, to some degree. You never know when you'll accidentally run across a new opportunity, a new ally, a new hire, or even a new job offer!

2.5. ORGANIZATIONAL CULTURE:
The skeleton holds the body together but you can't see it.

As the Top Manager, you need to know what your organization looks like from a functional perspective. What characteristics does it have in terms of its ability to respond to market conditions? What aspects need to be examined for weakness, what strengths need to be leveraged and exploited? What is the makeup of your staff and workforce? What policies, procedures, and strategies need to be utilized to realize your company's goals? Part of a thorough business analysis means precisely and accurately diagnosing all of these attributes. A championship football coach knows his team. He knows who the star players are. He knows how to situate best the members of the team such that they complement their strengths. He knows what kind of offense to run to mitigate individual weaknesses, and how to leverage the team makeup when up against different competitors. It is the only way the Top Manager is able to lead the team on to victory.

2.5.1. VERTICAL VS. HORIZONTAL:
Up, down, or Across, your process has to make sense.

Part of assessing your company's weaknesses is to seek to understand your organizational structure. Vertical organizations are often referred to as top-down management. In vertical organizations, employees adhere to a strict chain of command, and specific responsibilities are clearly defined. The leader at the top sets the vision and direction of the company.

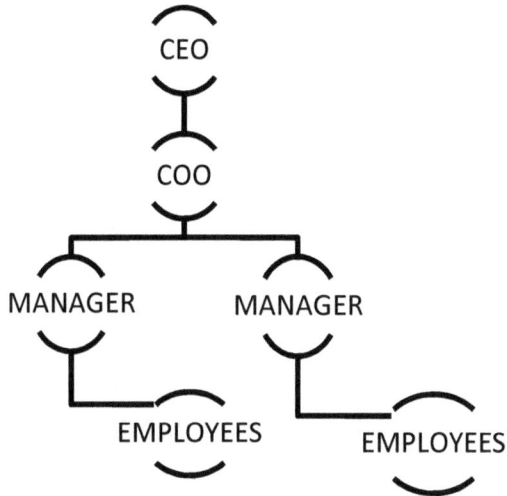

Horizontal organizations are generally less positioned to promote efficiency and the mechanisms by which the information that is processed can be ineffective. Many partnerships are horizontal by nature, because giving up ultimate authority to a sole member is at times a non-starter.

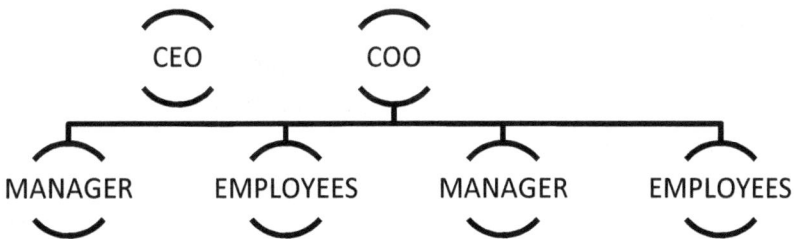

Let's explore the perils of this structure...

Think of two brothers who decide one day to open a business to sell cars. They both come in as equal partners in this new business. The doors are open, cars are shining on the lot, an advertising campaign is in full effect, and customers are starting to show up. When these two eager brothers started this business, an "efficient organizational framework" was the farthest from their mind. They were excited, they got a plan, and they both agreed that each could take charge of specific aspects of the business. They also realized that they were blood related and any future dispute will be resolved peacefully within the "tight" circle. Their bond is too strong and no disagreement could shake their foundation. For this reason, "We could be both the Boss, and can co-manage efficiently this business".

Fast-forward six months. It's very cold outside. The economy is bad and people nationwide are losing their jobs left and right. Money is getting tighter because cars are not selling. Some of the sales people are starting to use more aggressive tactics in order to sell. Other sales people are starting to leave early because they want to dedicate their afternoons to search for part-time jobs.

The Sales Manager wants to change the configuration of the lot. He wants to have more used cars in inventory because their target market cannot afford expensive cars anymore. One brother agrees with the new proposed direction. The other brother disagrees because he believes that selling anything other than brand new cars will compromise the brand equity they have worked so hard to build. His approach: "We just have to live through the rest of this recession; after all, it can't last forever". Regardless of positions, bills are starting to go unpaid. Sales people are starting to leave, and business is getting slower by the day. People are starting to take sides. This requires immediate action. However, we have two alpha males dead stuck on their position. They don't have to show deference or concede their positions. They are both the "Boss". IT IS A HORIZONTAL NIGHTMARE. They are both in charge at the same time. After a few weeks of avoiding bill collectors and because of high stress and emotions, a fistfight almost broke-out between the brothers one day.

The Death Blow:

The accountant shows up one afternoon with the worst kind of bad news: "Boys, you have to shut this business down, file bankruptcy, and get your stuff out of the building. Your debts are too overwhelming for you to stay afloat."

A classic example of the dangers that come with horizontal organizations. Sometimes, when an organization is going through tough times, a decision has to be made. Someone must have the authority to make it. Even if the decision is a bad one, at least something is happening. A standoff is never optimal. Horizontal organizations tend to produce standoffs when its "bosses" fundamentally disagree about a major business direction. Employees start to take sides, confusion takes over, and nobody knows what's what or who to follow. Inefficiencies start to prevail and the business faces certain failure.

In addition, horizontal companies are much harder to manage than vertical companies are, especially as the business grows, because the organization must foster the culture of SUPREME teamwork. Employees may also be less sure about their changing roles and responsibilities within the company, and project managers can be frustrated by their lack of definitive authority.

While we can agree that the depiction in the above example is very condemning of horizontal structures, we can also admit that in some instances, this structure could be acceptable. If an organization has multiple branches across the globe for example, then a combination of a horizontal and vertical structure may make sense if specific environments dictate it. However, if one has the option to choose between one and the other and if either is applicable, then it should NOT even be a discussion.

Insight:

From a management consulting standpoint, most organizations with a horizontal management structure are largely inefficient and broad confusion is the norm in daily operations. This is the reason why the majority of management consultants prefer to work with vertical structures. The systems and controls they would implement will have a better chance of being effective and applicable.

The Importance:

As a Top Manager, the prospect of managing a horizontal organization should frighten you. It is a big challenge even for the more advanced managers. It is very difficult. This is the reason why it is imperative to diagnose what structure you have in place as rapidly as possible. If the ensuing analysis depicts this horizontal structure, then be prepared to roll up your sleeves; you work load because you will to put in some serious work in order to operate a semi-efficient organization.

Insight:

Most employees do prefer a horizontal organization because it usually necessitates less accountability.

Strategy:

In Section 3, you will be introduced to the specific systems you can put into practice to install a vertical composition even if the verdict is "horizontal".

2.5.2. INCENTIVE PROGRAMS:

Lip Service will get old fast.

During this analysis, you have to determine the process by which your employees are rewarded for optimum performance and how they advance through the ranks of your organization. For example, you have to figure out the amount of steps required for a "worker bee" to attain a mid-level position and all the way to a senior level capacity.

THE IMPORTANCE:

You probably have heard of the following expressions: "Great organizational atmosphere", or "Employee satisfaction". One of the major contributing factors to a good organizational vibe is the clarity and honesty in place outlining the promotion process of an employee. As Abraham Maslow's Hierarchy of Needs describes, everyone wants to attain a respectable status to achieve some degree of self-actualization. In other words, people have a natural desire to accomplish something; in an organization, this will manifest itself in a given employee's pursuit of promotion and recognition. If the promotion process is too cumbersome to understand and too subjective to make it believable, rest assured that many in your company are sending out their resumes every day. If you prioritize this analysis, you will quickly have many partners in your organization. They will work hard to help you accomplish your goals. In the next section, you will learn how to install simple and efficient incentive programs for your employees.

2.6. STANDARD PROCEDURES:

Rules are as good as the means to enforcing them.

Standard procedures constitute the rules and guidelines an organization uses to perform its daily functions. Standard procedures are either written in manuals or reinforced verbally throughout an organization. In theory, the principal goal of a standard procedure is to ease the operational flow by facilitating the managerial functions of every department in an organization.

Insight:

Most standard procedures are usually flawed in concept and therefore, difficult to execute. Standard procedures are often constructed without outlining the actual processes to execute them.

In the analysis process, you must determine the following:

2.6.1. FEASIBILITY:

If something is unreasonable, why try it?

Many incompetent leaders will wake up one day and decide to write many rules and regulations and classify them as standard procedures. However, they are followed haphazardly when these leaders fail to outline the mechanisms of implementation in detail. In essence, these standard procedures never had a chance to make it into the workflow process. These managers failed to consider the feasibility issues with each of the standard procedures.

They are the following:

EXECUTION FACTOR:

Many employees do not follow standard procedures because they may lack the skill set required to perform the assigned responsibility. Let us assume for example that COMPANY SUPERTOP has established an accounting standard procedure requiring an employee to complete a complex financial operation at the end of each month. Let us also assume that the employee responsible for this task lacks the expertise to carry out complex financial transactions. Do you believe that this standard procedure will be followed? Of course not! The employee will only do as able. Essentially, this standard procedure was not realistic in its conception.

RESOURCE FACTOR:

In some cases, a standard procedure may require a resource that a company does not possess. This resource may be as simple as a document scanner or as complex as a network server. It could be the lack of a competent administrative staff member, or a permit or license, or even a bigger office space. Resource assessment should be a major factor to consider before developing any organizational policy.

TRANSFERABILITY:

Large organizations will typically have multiple branches across many regions and sometimes countries. However, only one set of uniform standard procedures may exist for all branches. They are usually produced by the executive members located in the main office or headquarters.

Here is the problem:

Because of regional differences, it could be impractical to institute an unvarying set of rules applicable to all branches. What works in region A may be irrelevant in region B and thus, not *transferable.*

Many top leaders in large organizations are hesitant to relinquish authority to branch managers. This compulsion to centralize "power" is the motivation, and branch managers aren't even permitted to formulate smarter methods of operation. These micromanagers are fearful of losing control. For this reason, the larger organizations are always prime suspects for having ineffective, non-applicable, or non-transferrable standard procedures across many branches.

2.6.2. CONTROL SYSTEM:
You need a firewall to prevent a breach of protocol.

The control system remains the main area of concern to any standard procedure. Basically, a standard procedure is only as good as its **enforceability system**. A control system is the force that will prevent an ill-advised action to take place. It restrains an employee for example, from moving through the next steps without first following the established protocol.

Consider the following two examples:

Example 1:

COMPANY SUPERTOP has a standard procedure requiring all checks submitted by customers to be deposited into the company's bank account by 4PM every day. The standard procedure reads as follows: "The accountant must deposit all checks submitted by customers by 4PM every day".

Here is the big question:

Will the accountant deposit all checks received from customers by 4PM every day?

Answer:

We do not know. What is lacking in this standard procedure is the assurance that it will be followed—the control system. On a side note, some companies will institute consequences when a standard procedure is not implemented. Ultimately, that is their control system. What if the accountant had a reasonable excuse to not deposit the check by 4PM? What if the check was received at 4:30

PM? What then? Should the accountant still get punished? Of course not! The check was received after the deadline.

Bottom Line:

There are usually "good" reasons why standard procedures are not followed. Under these circumstances, no one usually suffers consequences.

Possible Approach:

If the company REALLY wants this standard procedure to be followed, it should institute the following rule: "No employee is to receive a check from a customer after 3:30PM and all checks must be deposited by the accountant no later than 4PM every day". Now there is a control system. The chances of depositing all of the checks by 4PM are high. The accountant has ample time to make it to the bank by 4PM if it is located in a close proximity.

This simple control system assures the enforcement of this standard procedure. There should be no justifiable reason not to comply. Employees will have to say to customers: "Sorry Mr./Mrs./Ms. Customer, I can't take your check today because company policy prevents me from accepting checks after 3:30 PM. Can you please bring this check back tomorrow before 3:30 PM?" Even if this control system seems foolish and may result into loss of revenue, it guarantees that the rule will be followed. If checks are not deposited by 4PM, it is because someone accepted them after 3:30 PM and reprimand should follow.

Example 2:

COMPANY SUPERTOP standard procedure for inventory reads as follow: "The inventory manager must place an order for Product A when it reaches a limit of 20% on reserve".

Again, here are the main questions:

- Will the inventory manager place the order at exactly 20%?
- Are the necessary tools in place to meet this specific requirement?
- What if the inventory manager was tending to an emergency the day product A reached a limit of 20%? It is very likely that the order for Product A will not be placed.

Possible Approach:

COMPANY SUPERTOP should simply use an automated cyclical system that tracks the inventory level of each product. When the product reaches the predetermined critical level, a purchase order is printed automatically or emailed directly to the supplier. This type of technology exists to perform this action. In this case, this task should have never been enforced in the realm of standard procedures but in a computerized system where mathematical precision is essential. An average human being will not generally excel in this type of activity because it requires constant vigilance. This type of standard procedure lacks basic common sense.

This is a classic example of how organizations will institute shortsighted rules that will assure the constant failing of an employee.

2.7. EMPLOYEES' PERFORMANCE ANALYSIS:
Everyday excellence is at the core of continuous efficiency.

The purpose of this assessment is to measure the competence level as well as the efficiency of the employees when performing job duties. It also serves to enlighten possible areas of concern that may be toxic to the organization's smooth operation.

2.7.1. SPECIFIC JOB PERFORMANCE:
There is a million ways to do something, but only One best way.

For the purpose of this book, an employee is considered efficient when he or she can perform a job duty at least at a 90% capacity level. The remaining 10% is the room reserved for growth and "on the job training". Opinions regarding capacity level requirement may vary based on the industries, regions, and business types. However, our main goal is to build the best organization possible and therefore, only the highest standards should qualify as our barometers.

Method:

Tell the employees that you will evaluate their performance by asking ten specific questions about their job duties. It is worth noting that the quality of questions you ask will determine the accuracy of the rating process. You shouldn't ask general questions that could be answered with a lucky guess or convoluted vague response.

Insight:

Consider your questions ineffective if you must ask more than ten to rate the job performance of an employee.

For example, the following shouldn't be one of your questions: "Mr./Ms. Employee, tell me about your day as the bookkeeper?"

This is how the question should be asked: "Mr./Ms. employee, how do you perform end-of -the month reconciliations? This is a pinpoint question that will force the employee to answer in a specific nature.

Rating System:

An employee is considered effective if he or she can answer nine of the ten questions with EASE. Accordingly, anything less than ten is considered ineffective.

2.7.2. MINDSET:
Pay attention to things that are hidden in people's psyche.

The questions in this section serve to gauge the general atmosphere of the organization. In simple terms, you want to find the organizational tensions that may exist. As a bonus, these questions may also help to determine if the employees have a shared interest in the success of the organization. Again, the caliber of your questioning will be the deciding factor in gathering useful information. For example, do not ask: "Are you happy to work for this company?" Or, "What do you like the most about your job? Instead, you should ask: "What are the barriers preventing you from working effectively?" Or, "Who are the people in this organization negatively affecting the work atmosphere?"

As you can tell, the questions are presented in a negative manner and for a good reason. **During, this analysis, *you do not need to dwell on what is right but what is WRONG.*** Putting a laser focus on the negative forces that exist within your organization will prove to be a better use of your time rather than positive areas that require less immediate attention. During this psychological analysis, you are only looking for anger, tension, stress, annoyance, frustration, boredom, etc. Even more, you are looking any negative feeling between front-line employees and managers.

2.7.3. INTERNAL THIRST:

We all want something else.

As a manager, it is always to your benefit to know what your employees would like to achieve within your organization.

Insight:

In many companies, the top leaders will totally dismiss employees' internal thirst. In truth, they view employees as disposable tools utilized to only build wealth for their portfolios. You should never adopt this mentality because your employees will see right through it. To your loss, they will do only the minimum possible for your organization, which will hinder your growth process. If your employees believe that you seek their best interest, then they will work hard to help you accomplish your goals. To your benefit, it is a win-win working relationship. By genuinely pushing for their ascension and by defeating your natural thirst for wealth only, you will build a solid framework with dedicated partners prone to long-term success.

2.7.4. RELUCTANCE TO CHANGE:

Turtles do not win marathons... unless it is against other turtles.

Once this Business Analysis is complete, it is very likely that you will need to implement changes. For this reason, you must determine if your employees will accept with great enthusiasm the new structures you will institute. Understanding this reluctance to change in advance will help develop the necessary contingency plans.

Insight:

In many organizations, dramatic restructuring is a very scary proposition because most employees do not like change.

2.7.5. RESPONSIBILITY AND SUPERVISION:

Clarity will enlighten a dark tunnel.

More often than not, employees cannot outline their responsibilities with clarity and expected contribution to the company. The lack of an efficient organizational structure may cause their job duties to change on a consistent basis. Other employees strive to work hard and productively but lack the proper supervision. It is likely that during the analysis, they would project poor job performance. This is the toughest part when interviewing employees. You must substantiate if the lack of clear responsibilities and effective supervision made them inefficient. This is the time when your analytical skills will be put to the test.

SAMPLE EMPLOYEE'S ASSESSMENT QUESTIONNAIRE :

EMPLOYEE'S NAME:	TITLE
PATRICK MORRIS	BOOKKEEPER
MANAGER'S NAME:	DEPARTMENT:
MARY SMITH	ACCOUNTING

JOB PERFORMANCE:

1. Describe your process for monthly reconciliations? Pass ☐ Fail ☐
2. Describe your process for managing accounts receivable? Pass ☐ Fail ☐
3. Describe your process for managing accounts payables? Pass ☐ Fail ☐
4. Describe your process for managing monthly bills? Pass ☐ Fail ☐
5. Describe your process for developing financial reports? Pass ☐ Fail ☐
6. Describe your process for handling online payments? Pass ☐ Fail ☐
7. Describe your process for filing financial documents? Pass ☐ Fail ☐
8. Describe your process for managing our general ledger? Pass ☐ Fail ☐
9. Describe your process for processing weekly payroll? Pass ☐ Fail ☐
10. Describe your process for managing Clients' invoices? Pass ☐ Fail ☐

MINDSET:

1. What are the barriers preventing you from working effectively?
2. Who are the people negatively affecting the work atmosphere?
3. What is holding you back from over-exceling?
4. How flawed are the systems we are using?
5. Name three weaknesses your manager possesses?

INTERNAL THIRST

1. Are you looking for a better wage and incentives programs?
2. Are you looking to get promoted?
3. Are you being recognized for your hard work?
4. Do you want to take part of meetings held by senior managers?
5. What are your short and long-term goals?

RELUCTANCE TO CHANGE:

1. Are you open to a change in your job description?
2. Would you be open to being reassigned to another department?
3. We may install new systems next week; do you want to lead their implementation?

RESPONSIBILITY AND SUPERVISION:

1. Do you understand your job duties clearly?
2. What in your responsibilities you think is too much or unfair?
3. Do you need more or less supervision?
4. How effective is your supervisor? Can you do her job better?

2.8. GOALS & OBJECTIVES:

Knowing what you want is knowing who you are?

This analysis is about you—the TOP MANAGER. You need to cultivate the ability to be honest with yourself and uncompromising with your own personal assessment and expectations. You will need this mindset in order to figure out the following . . .

2.8.1. ACHIEVABILITY:

Be realistic and honest with yourself.

Many leaders will make it a habit to set their sights on unachievable goals. Without debate, everybody has the inalienable right to dream big and strive for greatness. Furthermore, hard work and perseverance should predict one's expected success and theoretically, no boundaries should exist. As stated earlier, you should always **shoot for the moon**, as long it is within your human ability. This means some of your big goals may be impossible to achieve. You can't let other people define your goals for you. However, does it make sense sometimes to seek unrealistic goals?

For example, should the leader of a small company with revenues of only $100,000 have as a goal to dominate the global market within the next three years of operation and earn $10 Billion in revenues? In all honesty, what are the chances that this would happen? Without being too pessimistic, not many have done it. The odds of this goal becoming a reality are very limited. Write down every goal you have for yourself and your company, and in good conscience assess whether they are achievable. On the flip side, can you also set higher goals if the ones you currently have are too weak, slim, and not bold enough?

2.8.2. EXPERTISE:

Some people are successful for a reason.

Simply, do you have the expertise required to achieve your goals. In the example described above, do you have the intellectual ability to lead a multinational organization? In addition, do you understand all of the dynamics of the world market? Alternatively, are you well connected to build worldwide strategic partnerships? Essentially, you must always determine if the knowledge you possess matches the goals and objectives you are setting for yourself.

2.8.3. ATTRACTION:

Be smart about what you will offer and your returns will shine.

Are the products/services you sell, attractive and needed? Once more, will the markets seek them? Are there supply chains available to fulfill this goal?

2.8.4. NECESSITY:

Don't get stuck to ideology, or you may always swim around mud.

Can you accomplish the **same level of success** without setting unrealistic goals? Is staying regional your best choice for example? In this regard, you must truly examine the main purpose and intent behind the goal. Is it what's best for the business? Or, has personal aspiration or desire for prestige somehow influenced your choice? Again, it is important to be honest with yourself when determining the rationality of your goals.

2.8.5. CLARITY:

Goals & Objectives are like pepper and salt—different but complementary.

Many leaders will have goals that are not only confusing to them but to anyone trying to make sense of them. Perhaps they are trying to go in too many directions at once. Often these types of leaders lack a clear picture of where they want to be. They just have bits and pieces of the puzzle. Many illustrations exist to define goals and objectives. For our purpose however, goals and objectives are characterized as the following:

A goal is the final milestone comprised of multiple objectives.

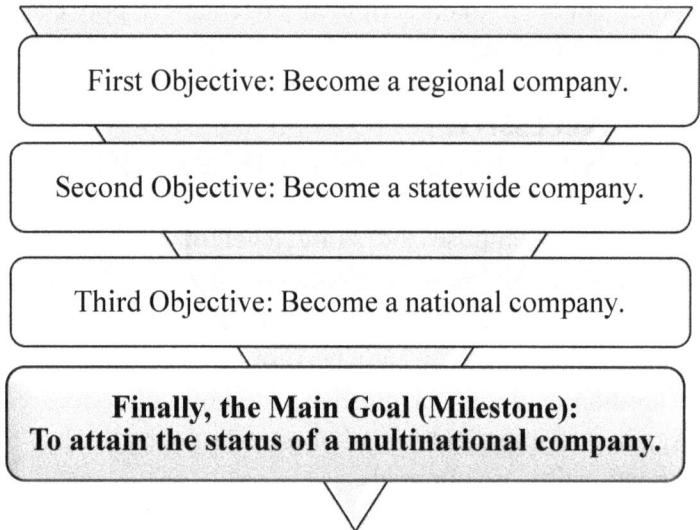

First Objective: Become a regional company.

Second Objective: Become a statewide company.

Third Objective: Become a national company.

**Finally, the Main Goal (Milestone):
To attain the status of a multinational company.**

SUCCESS

You want to reach the level and status of a multinational organization within the next three years—the final milestone or the GOAL.

To reach the final goal however, many intermediary goals need to be achieved first. They are the OBJECTIVES.

In this case, three objectives are required to reach one final goal. Each objective has its own strategies. When they are broken down using this model, then a goal is always easier to reach.

Insight:

Many intelligent leaders do not understand this very simple concept. They will consistently confuse goals and objectives. For this reason, their scattered brains will spin in multiple directions and they can never demonstrate with ease the process required to reach their destination.

2.9. MARKETING STRATEGY:

To connect: Hit them hard—Hit them enough—Hit them good.

For the purpose of this analysis, we will use a standard and popular model called the "5 Ps" with a slight managerial economics twist. The 5 Ps are: Product, Place, Price, Promotion, and People.

Insight:

The 5 Ps are also referred to as the "Marketing Mix".

2.9.1. PRODUCT:

Understand where you stand and you may know where to lean.

Background:

It is important to learn the types of products organizations offer in order to develop the best possible marketing strategies. For this reason, we will cover some basic economics principles that explain these variations. In Economics, a tangible product is often referred to as a "Good".

Suggestion:

You should invest some time learning basic economic theories, especially in the field of Microeconomics. Many people tend to dismiss the value of studying Economics. Some even refer to Economics as: "common sense made difficult." Actually, it is not. Economics will help you understand better the dynamics between markets, consumer behaviors, international trade, and much more.

2.9.2. NORMAL VS. INFERIOR GOOD (PRODUCT):

Everything we offer has Benefits and Consequences.

Normal Good:

In Economics, a good is normal when its demand increases as the consumer income increases. Cars and clothes are very good examples. The more money a consumer has to spend, the more money he or she will to spend on a new vehicle or wardrobe.

Insight:

"Necessity" goods are types of normal goods. The fluctuations of income for a consumer have no substantial impact on the demand—milk for a baby is a perfect example of a necessity good. The consumer will buy milk regardless of the fluctuations in income.

Inferior Good:

A good is Inferior when its demand decreases as the consumer income increases. Canned food and bus riding are perfect examples. With more money, a consumer may want to buy fresh food rather than cheaper, lower quality canned foods. Additionally, as the consumer's income rises, he or she will, in all likelihood, opt to drive an automobile in favor of riding the bus.

2.9.3. SUBSTITUTES VS. COMPLEMENTS:

Decisions are all about choices.

Substitute Good:

Substitute goods are purchased to replace a consumer's products once environmental and economic changes take precedent. For example, a consumer may decide to replace a broom for a vacuum cleaner. Another classic example is to substitute a home phone for a cellular phone.

Insight:

The act of changing brands is considered "substituting" as well.

Complement Good:

Complement goods are purchased to satisfy the enjoyment or usability of another product. For example, a DVD player is a complementary good because it needs a television to be useful.

2.9.4. READY VS. IN-THE-MIX GOODS:

Every strategy will bear some results.

Ready Good:

Ready goods can be used by consumers the moment they buy it—a television for example. Most of the "ready" goods are sold to final consumers.

In-the-Mix Good:

These goods require an intermediary production process to become a final product. Chemicals are good examples. To make laundry detergent for instance, a manufacturing company may need to buy chemicals from another company to produce the final product.

2.9.5. GENERAL STRATEGY:

Every road will lead to a destination.

Now that you understand the basic principles that encompass products, let's outline the possible strategies to consider.

Normal, Inferior, and Necessity:

From a strategic perspective, normal and necessity goods are the ones every company should offer.

The Reason:

They are less sensitive to economic shifts and downturns. If a company is selling baby milk for example, then we can assume that its consumer base will always exist. Babies need milk. People need to eat. This is the reason why most grocery stores can persevere during the harshest economic recessions. However, you should also acknowledge that normal and necessity goods typically bear low margins. A company must sell large amounts of these goods to remain profitable. In essence, leveraging "economies of scale" by spreading fixed costs across a greater number of sales will help to solidify a company's profitability.

Strategy:

If your company offers normal, inferior and necessity goods, then you should focus your analysis on the history of volume sold. If there are considerable fluctuations, then there is probably reason for concern. Your sales need to either increase on a consistent basis or remain at a steady rate.

2.9.6. SUBSTITUTES AND COMPLEMENTS:

A plan of action is simple to develop if you know where to start.

A company offering substitute and complement products will usually operate in a very volatile environment. As you have noticed, there are multiple TV brands for a consumer to fancy. In this type of market, companies are engaged in price wars and aggressive marketing tactics to stay afloat. Accordingly, they are the ones that will feel the highest brunt of economic shifts and recessions.

Strategy:

If your company offers substitute and complement products, then you should focus your analysis on the existing competition as well as the current strategy in place for facing future economic shifts.

2.9.7. READY AND IN-THE-MIX:

Avenues are roads with lights.

Strategy:

Along with an analysis of the history of volume sold, you should also perform a thorough analysis of the current supply chain. A company offering Ready and In–the-Mix goods must have multiple avenues to distribute its products/services.

2.9.8. PLACE:

The Return On Investment is the Harvest in a farm?

The "Place" usually refers to the location of operation. This analysis serves to find the efficiency of the current place strategy. In essence, the operational benefits enjoyed from the current location.

The following are some of the questions you should investigate:

- Is the location optimal for serving the current client base? For instance, does it make sense to operate in the eastern region when most of the customers are located in the western region?
- Were tax strategies in the discussions when deciding to operate in a state or country?
- What are the possible offshoring and outsourcing strategies?
- Are the distributions and supply channels optimized with the current location?
- What are the current difficulties the company is facing because of its Place strategy?
- How is the Place strategy affecting the operational efficiency and effectiveness of the company?
- Is the growth of the company being hindered because of its current location(s)?
- How does the Place strategy fit in the overall business plan?
- Will a growth strategy require a change in Place?

2.9.9. PRICE:

> If what you have is precious, everyone will buy it.

When it comes to the Price analysis, there are two areas to focus on: Pricing Method and Pricing Objective.

Pricing Method:

A formula needs to solve a problem with a mathematical precision.

Strategy:

From the analysis of your current pricing strategy, you must establish in details its contribution to the gain or loss of profitability.

The pricing method refers to the formula or technique used to set the value of a product/service. There are multiple pricing strategies available to businesses. However, the majority of companies use Cost-Plus Pricing, which simply adds a profit margin to the actual of cost of production. Other companies use a competitive pricing strategy, which simply matches the price of the closest competitor. Alternatively, some will use a dynamic pricing strategy, which revolves around the industry shifts, seasonal peaks, or outside economic factors.

Pricing Objective:

The following represent the most popular pricing objectives:

- Maximizing revenue
- Maximizing profits
- Remaining solvent
- Bankrupting competition

Strategy:

Develop a Cost/Benefit analysis for each for pricing objective before you put it into practice.

2.9.10. PROMOTION:

How well can you say: "You want what I have"

The Promotion strategy is the driving force behind any marketing plan. During your analysis, you have to evaluate the following mediums:

Print Media:

Print Media usually comes in the form of postcards, newsletters, coupon books, etc. Print Media is becoming obsolete because of technology. Grocery stores, pizzerias, auto repair shops are some of the companies that still use this medium as a method for advertisement.

Strategy:

To analyze its effectiveness, utilize the Return On Investment (ROI) as your default standard. Therefore, you must compare the historical sales volume and the amount invested in this medium.

The bottom Line: a positive correlation is required to justify the continued usage of this medium.

Social Media:

Social Media is the newest avenue to promoting businesses. These days, it is in most cases, paramount to have a strong online presence. Because of the explosion of technology, the standards when it comes to searching and buying products have changed. New social media platforms, trends, habits, and demographics are forming the foundation for a paradigm shift in the way companies do business. Properly managing a company's web presence WILL spell the difference between success and failure. These issues in no way constitute a passing fad. In the first few years of the 2000's, the internet boom was still in its relative youth ... perhaps even infancy, depending on how one might define it. At that point, there were dozens of internet startups that had great ideas, and many of them were funded solely on novelty. Many people began to recognize the classic prerequisites of a "bubble", and saw the landscape to be overpopulated by companies that *were* indeed fads. Then the bubble burst. It resulted in a recession. As a result, the American investing public was left with a bad taste in its mouth when it came to internet companies.

So no longer is it just novelties like interactive websites, e-mail campaigns, webinars, e-cards, and connecting with some of your customers online. The market has established a new standard for the methods of doing business. In the late 1990's, only major companies and computer experts had websites of even remedial quality. This was back when professional developers could charge virtually tens of thousands of dollars for a single website ... in some cases even as much as $100,000. Now you can find starving programmers and developers that are willing to put together a professional quality website for a few hundred bucks.

It is clear that this is the wave of the future. Businesses who neglect to stay abreast of the ever-accelerating developments will be left in the dust. So you, as the Top Manager will have to choose how, when, and how much your company needs to invest in this area. Do you need to outsource some of your search engine optimization functions? Do you need to consider elevating your prerequisite credentials during the hiring process? Even for non-technical staff? How often and how much money and time should you spend on updating, revamping, and overhauling your approach to web presence? Complacency breeds inefficiency, especially in today's breakneck speed of doing business.

In addition, your analysis should not forget that there is a REASON behind your foray into and involvement with a web presence. So many companies put an attractive webpage together that does nothing more than serve as backup for a business card. Perhaps this might not be as effective as it should be for a business. Is your web presence drawing in NEW customers? How are your organic search results on the major search engine platforms? What is your click-through rate? Do you need to engage in relationships with affiliate advertisers?

These are all questions that are beyond the scope of this discussion, but warrant serious consideration. We bring them up to illustrate the potential pitfalls that many companies face when developing their own space online. In other words, don't just create a website that replicates info elsewhere and leave it to be swallowed up by the black holes and cobwebs at the far end of the internet. Instead, actively engage your customers and prospective clients through this medium. Make the time and expenditure meaningful. Carefully analyze what sort of returns, or even business buzz these actions are generating. Basically, don't just spend money on something because it's the thing to do.

Strategy:

Again, the main standard here is the ROI. Your analysis must determine if your online presence is not only generating leads but also resulting in sales. If there isn't an existing system to evaluate its efficacy, then the entire strategy may be useless.

Major Insight:

A strategy is a good as its means to analyzing its success.

Indirect Approaches:

They include direct face-to-face interactions with customers, community partnerships, networking, trade shows, conferences, sponsorships, etc. Indirect approaches are the grey area of promotion because evaluating their success is very difficult.

Insight:

Many marketers argue that the intrinsic value of this marketing tactic is to build "goodwill". Still, some mechanisms to evaluate success must be established.

Strategy:

You should certainly calculate the costs associated with indirect approaches. If cost control is an issue in your organization for example, then you will know where to cut first.

2.9.11. PEOPLE:

Your Sales force is your most valuable resource when selling.

People are the marketing staff in an organization. Your analysis should include the following:

Technique:

You will seek to discover the methods and processes used to attract and sell to customers. For example, if aggressive techniques are used to close a client; then you must answer the "if not" questions. Simply put, what are the cost and benefits associated with the usage of a specific sales technique?

Performance:

In this analysis, you want to find out how successful your sales people are individually and as group. The performance evaluation in this case is very simple—Just match the direct sales with time spent in marketing activities.

Desire:

In many firms, there are staff members who work in the marketing department but lack the desire or interest in it. Either they were pushed to work in this department or they just needed a job. As you suspect, selling should be about passion, seeking to continually best yourself, and have a sincere thirst to become "number one". For your organization to remain successful in its overall strategy, everyone in the marketing staff must truly cherish their job with the utmost zeal.

2.10. OPERATIONAL SYSTEMS & CONTROLS (OSCS):

Every successful organization needs a well-oiled machine.

As stated earlier, OSCs are the engine of an organization. In the next chapter, you will learn how to build the best OSCs in the world. In this section, we will just outline two basic concepts for the evaluation process if you have some systems and controls in place:

2.10.1. EFFICIENCY:

You can do it better every day.

Here, the goal is to find out if the company's resources are used optimally. Thus, are the OSCs contributing to a smooth workflow process? You should refer back to the Comparative Cost Analysis (CCA) to assess the efficiency of the OSCs. Again, multiple fluctuations of costs represent a lack of an efficient control system.

Strategy:

Use your findings in the CCA to rate the efficiency of each OSC. Consider any OSC inefficient if the cost fluctuations are significant throughout the analyzed timeframe.

2.10.2. VERSATILITY:

Always think of Growth before you decide on anything.

When instituting OSCs, a good leader will take into account the possible growth of the organization. Hence, the OSCs must be flexible enough to sustain a bigger infrastructure.

Insight:

The process of organizational restructuring is tough especially for the average employee. Rigid OSCs will make the transition even more burdensome.

Strategy:

The creation of versatile OSCs should be a top priority if you were to diagnose the existence of rigid OSCs in your organization.

2.11. FINANCIAL STRUCTURE:

Money is Money.

2.11.1. RAPIDITY:

Get it sooner and you can invest it faster.

The decision-making process is always easier if the top leadership is able to review swiftly the financial information of the company. For example, it should be unacceptable to wait weeks just to receive reports about the cash flow status, actual payables and receivables, return on investments, etc.

2.11.2. ACCURACY:

Numbers never lie.

Many leaders will confess that they consistently doubt the accuracy of the financial reports they receive from their financial staff. This happens with even the largest companies. In most cases, the lack of a universal computation method is the main culprit. For example, one department may allocate a specific expenditure as a fixed while another as a variable cost.

The Result:

A flawed combined report that is useless for any financial analysis.

Process:

Compare the reports of two different departments or units and look for variations of formulas. The slightest difference you find is a reason to doubt the accuracy of the financial reporting system.

2.11.3. AUTOMATION:

Machines were invented for a reason—to simplify our lives.

In today's business environment, an efficient financial structure requires almost full automation. Daily cash flows and current inventory reports are good examples. It is almost impossible for these reports to be accurate dependably unless a systematic methodology is in place.

Strategy:

Outline the critical reports needed in the organization and figure out which are automated. A satisfactory grade requires 90% automation on all of these reports.

2.11.4. SCALABILITY:

Think you the future before you make today's decisions.

Fundamentally, you want to determine if the current financial structure will be applicable if the company growths. Furthermore, is there a system in place that could gather all of the financial information received from multiple locations and summarize it into one conclusive report?

2.12. ENTITY STRUCTURE & TAX STRATEGY:

Plan First, Enjoy it later.

2.12.1. ENTITY STRUCTURE:

Ask questions, ask again, and you may learn something.

You do not have to be an expert in this field to ask the basic questions. The generally accepted purpose of an entity structure is to shelter the assets of the company.

The following are the most important questions to ask:

- Was asset protection in the discussion when the company was formed?
- What is the current strategy for sheltering assets?
- What does the current liability insurance cover?
- What is the current valuation of the company?
- What are the exit strategies in place for the owners?
- What is the succession plan in place?

2.12.2. TAX MINIMIZATION STRATEGY:

Reducing what you owe is increasing what you have.

The goal of any tax strategy is minimize its cost—that is, how much a company pays annually in state and federal taxes.

Insight:

The bigger companies will hire highly competent tax strategists because they understand that the less you pay in taxes, the more there are for profits. They view taxes as a controllable expense tied directly to profitably.

There are multiple tax strategies available to companies. Here are some:

- Systematic amortization and depreciation models
- Creation of multiple entities
- Scheduled dividends allocations

Insight:

Your goal in this analysis is to discover only if asset protection and tax minimization strategies are currently in place and being implemented. If you can't get clear answers, do not lose hope because there are many tax experts always looking for work.

SECTION III -
BUILD THE BEST
STRUCTURE:

By this point, you're well on your way toward acquiring the Mindset of the Top Manager. You've been given an overview of the requisite tools needed to master the Business Analysis. You're ready to change your company from the inside out. You're ready to take control and make a meaningful and lasting impact, because the Top Manager is all about the Bottom Line. Now it is time to achieve yet another milestone; building the best organizational structure or TAKING A COMPANY OVER THE TOP.

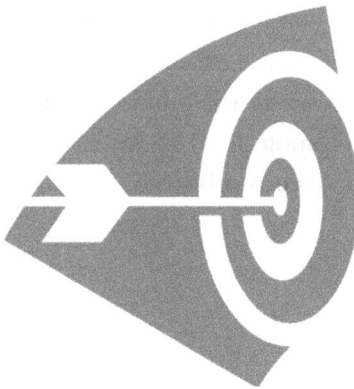

The following model has proven to being the prime template for the most successful companies. It promotes efficiency, simplicity, control, sustainability, profitability, and, most importantly, wealth accumulation. This infrastructure is applicable to any organization regardless of industry and size.

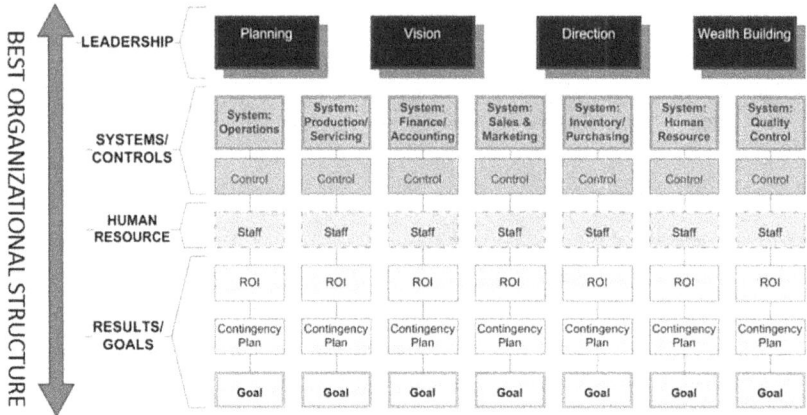

		Planning		Vision		Direction		Wealth Building	
LEADERSHIP									
SYSTEMS/ CONTROLS	System: Operations	System: Production/ Servicing	System: Finance/ Accounting	System: Sales & Marketing	System: Inventory/ Purchasing	System: Human Resource	System: Quality Control
	Control	Control	Control	Control	Control	Control	Control
HUMAN RESOURCE	Staff	Staff	Staff	Staff	Staff	Staff	Staff
	ROI	ROI	ROI	ROI	ROI	ROI	ROI
RESULTS/ GOALS	Contingency Plan	Contingency Plan	Contingency Plan	Contingency Plan	Contingency Plan	Contingency Plan	Contingency Plan
	Goal	Goal	Goal	Goal	Goal	Goal	Goal

BEST ORGANIZATIONAL STRUCTURE

As seen in the graph, the organizational structure is composed of four vertical and progressive elements: Leadership, Systems & Controls, Human Resource, and Results & Goals. Each segment starting from the top facilitates the efficient implementation of the next one below all the way to the ultimate GOAL. They are strategically linked so to promote the two necessities for a smooth operation: **Efficiency and Accountability.**

Now Let us take a closer look at each part of this framework:

3.1. LEADERSHIP:

Your priorities are where it all begins.

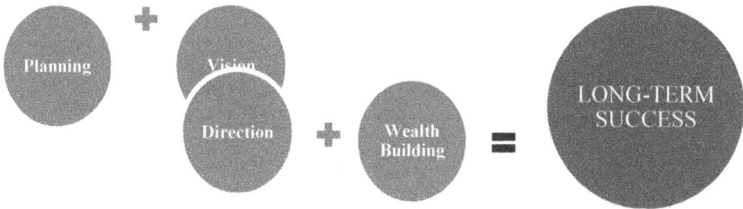

Planning + **Vision** / **Direction** + **Wealth Building** = **LONG-TERM SUCCESS**

TOP MANAGER'S RESPONSIBILITIES

The model begins FIRST with the most essential components of Effective Leadership. **Planning, Vision, Direction, and Wealth Building** should be the prime responsibilities of the Top Manager. In fact, these are your lifelines. For the rest of this book, consider those four components analogous to your food, water, shelter, and exercise you need to survive healthily. This is because these elements are crucial to your survival. So let us reiterate ...

The Top manager who focuses only on Planning, Vision, Direction, and Wealth Building will be ready to tackle future contingencies and secure a chance for long-term profitability.

No other task, regardless of perceived importance, should prevail atop these fundamentals. All other elements of organizational success are pinned or tied inextricably to these four concepts; use them as your guiding principles and you will *take your company OVER THE TOP*. Leaders of less successful organizations usually lack the discipline to stay on course in regards to this basic approach. They won't stick to the program. Pseudo-important tangents often take precedence, and the ineffectual manager loses sight of big picture priorities in favor of less important tasks. When you do in effect stick to this principle, you automatically gain an advantage over those less grounded in this framework. Ahead of the game in comparison to those who lack your focus on effective prioritization. You may recall this concept in Section 1 during our discussion of delegating the workload.

Throughout the year, a distracted manager will take part in countless petty activities while the major job duties go ignored. People often subconsciously use this as a tactic to avoid more pressing issues and urgent responsibilities. It's like the manager who buries his head in the sand by taking inventory of the supplies closet as a measure to address cost overruns and budget shortages. Even worse, he might wastes two people's time by supervising the office manager while this task is being performed.

You could compare this to the captain of an ocean liner who will set the ship on a basic course, and proceed to run down to the engine room to make sure the crew is handling the boiler controls properly. He then rushes to the engineer to confirm that all of the pistons, furnaces, pumps, and cylinders are in proper working order. Next, he double-checks the cargo, because he wants to confirm everything was loaded and properly secured. In the meantime, the ship has veered off track considerably. Upon his return to the helm, the ship's captain must make major adjustments to return the ship along its plotted course.

Corrective actions are the best-case scenario for the scatterbrained captain, who in this scenario managed to avoid an iceberg collision while away from the wheel. The ship and its crew may wind up with the good fortune of arriving at their next port of call, but odds are they will have spent a considerable amount of time off the beaten path. The same goes for the shortsighted manager who spends too much time hovering over employees' process oriented tasks. Every moment he spends away from his manager chair is another mile his ship deviates from its designed course. These managers somehow miss the fact that the majority of their burdens are caused by their failure to assume fully their prime responsibilities.

The Firehouse Phenomenon:

In truth, many leaders behave as firefighters rather than managers. They spend the majority of their days putting fires out (solving business problems) rather than creating an efficient platform as described above. These types of managers end up operating in a bubble, oblivious to the true cause of all of the fires that need extinguishing. These managers are unable to assimilate or comprehend the essence of leading an organization from the top in lieu of the bottom or in the between.

3.1.1. PLANNING:
Being on TOP means to prioritize preparation.

Let's face it; you are not going to get anywhere if you do not plan properly. From the most complex projects to the simplest tasks are immutably more successful when accompanied by or organized by way of a coherent plan. Every structure begins with a blueprint. With that in mind, compare *long-term organizational planning* to the to-do list you write up at the beginning of each day, week, or month. If you're managing your time and tasks efficiently, you probably address easier the dreaded to-do list in some form or another.

THERE ARE 84,600 SECONDS IN THE DAY.

The Manager who succeeds is the one who uses these seconds most wisely.

An effective workweek is managed by a periodic to-do list. A to-do list is always part of a more encompassing big-picture time management scheme. There have been enough books on this subject for it not to be necessary to expand on here. For our discussion, we'll assume that you have implemented or have access to a suitable method of planning. We'll also assume that effective planning and time-management are of paramount importance. We know this to be true. Time management is invariably tied with effective planning. The two concepts are reliant upon one another.

The only way to use each second *wisely* is through clear, concise, and effective planning. Generally, you look to get an idea of what major projects or assignments need to be completed in a given month. In effect, these are your GOALS. To break this down for further consumption, you might allocate certain items on your itinerary every Monday morning into easily digestible chunks for

the week. These are essentially your OBJECTIVES. The process level commotion lists you generate each morning help you stay on track to meet these goals. Organizational goals function much in the same fashion. This is a great comparison to how one would efficiently plan the company's goals and objectives.

Examples of efficient planning are:

- Setting larger picture objectives for long-term targets
- Setting objectives to serve as the milestones toward goals
- Strategizing for opportunities to integrate in new markets
- Planning for future challenges and market shifts

Now that you have decided how you are going to structure your plans to meet your targets and aspirations, it is time to look at some planning oriented specifics.

Five critical questions when it comes to planning:

QUESTION:	ANSWER:
1. How often should Planning occur?	Daily
2. What is subject to Planning?	Everything
3. Who should engage in Planning?	Everyone, especially the top Leadership
4. What happens if Planning does not occur often?	Future sustainability very unlikely
5. WHAT IS THE BEST PLANNING METHOD?	1. Set priorities 2. Brainstorm possible strategies 3. Develop systematic Cost-Benefit Analyses 4. Pick the best the strategy 5. Develop a comprehensive schedule of implementation 6. Set objectives 7. Set goals 8. Get started

3.1.2. VISION:

Take seriously the picture you take of yourself.

The vision is more in-house and it is where and when a company sees itself in the future. A well-developed vision statement can become a strong incentive for the employees to work harder. A typical vision statement will paint a picture for the future that is more than likely, better than the current one. In essence, people like to work hard for something they consider, has potential. A vision statement is also a living, breathing organism that can be updated and amended as internal and external factors evolve. It is dynamic. It can grow and change along with your company … but it should always be done with a clear picture of the desired result. This is where many corporate vision statements are deficient, as they are not drafted with an honest assessment of where the company is going. They are just something fancy to put on the wall for customers to see. Again, let us point out that the purpose of the vision statement is to provide direction for the company itself; not to show off. The latter is a secondary concern. So be honest, thoughtful, and realistic in your creation of the vision and involve the vision's most important stakeholders … the employees. They will be able to give you some powerfully valuable input in this task. Allocate some time throughout your week to think about your vision. It will help you to understand the reason you are working so hard. It is essentially your internal motivation to get out of your bed every day and push on for the THING you want to have or accomplish.

Review:

The vision has to be attainable rather than being a senseless statement that lacks the credibility.

3.1.3. DIRECTION:

A road well-travelled is a road well lit.

Along with a plan, you're going to need a map. You need to know the shortest path between you and your destination. You're also *going to need a compass*, because you may not know what direction you need to point yourself before you start walking. The Direction represents the specific routes to travel on to reach the Vision. The Direction strategy should be clear, achievable, and systematically adjusted as situations and events evolve over time. Just like road atlases eventually evolved into GPS on your smartphone. Your Direction strategy needs to evolve as well.

Insight:

Setting the Direction can sometimes turn into a tricky proposition because of the potential risk. It may require an extreme amount of audacity from the leader.

3.1.4. WEALTH BUILDING:

Riches can do a whole lot of good.

Every leader should focus on accumulating wealth over the life of a company. When it comes to the stakeholders, building wealth is what interests them the most because it guarantees rise of stock value. Many incompetent leaders equate revenue generation with wealth accumulation. In fact, they may not affect considerably each other. The purpose of revenues is to cover costs with the hope of retaining a portion described as profits. The profits pay for dividends, R&D, new acquisitions, etc. Wealth is in a different realm. It really needs to be built-in to the cost structure. Saving and investing wisely are the only real ways to generate and maintain WEALTH. In this regard, personal finance tactics are not so dissimilar from managing the wealth accounts of a major corporation.

To accumulate wealth, the Top Manager focuses primarily on the following:

- Retained Earnings From Profits
- Effectively Managing Receivables
- "Hard Assets" (Buildings And Equipment)
- Large Client Base
- Long-Term Contracts
- Intangibles (Patents, Goodwill, Trade Secrets, Etc.)

One can see clearly that this is a separate issue from driving current term revenues. Revenues don't mean a thing without effective wealth management. Otherwise, your company will end up like the spendthrift who drives a Porsche, but can't afford to fill the gas tank.

WEALTH BUILDING
is the essential path to long-term prosperity

Therefore, for the arena of wealth building, we will focus on the factors covered in the bulleted list above. The combination of all of these elements will increase the value of an organization. Amassing this wealth guarantees long-term sustainability of an organization because it becomes a lifeline during economic recessions and downturns. Everyone can make hay while the sun shines. However, if you waited until August to plant your seeds, you're going to have a long winter.

When tough times strike and we all tighten up our belts, the lack of a steady stream of revenue will need to be supplemented by a stockpile of wealth. In this case, the strength of wealth becomes even more of a necessity for survival. A good leader will never fall into the trap of believing that strong revenues are the essence of sustenance. You have to feed your wealth machine as much as you feed your business. Otherwise, it won't be able to return the favor in your business' time of need. Always have a backup plan with a backup plan.

Insight:

When the Big 3 automakers in Detroit suddenly experienced drastic downturns in demand and production capacity in the early to mid-2000s, there were many lives affected by the changes to the business environment. The ripple effect extended far beyond General Motors, Ford, and Chrysler. For instance, the sharp decrease in demand for new automobiles instantly ruined the businesses of many auto-dealers. This had the chain reaction of killing revenues for the myriad of companies that executed financing services that facilitated credit sales at the many dealerships. Thousands of dealerships across the country shuttered their doors throughout the decade. GM was one of the most profitable companies in business history ... and then almost went BANKRUPT. Even after accepting Billions from the US federal government. That is B-I-L-L-I-O-N-S.

That's fine, we might say. There's no way they could have anticipated the dozens of tragedies and problems that befell the automaker behemoth during the first decade of the 21st century. In fact, we can make any excuse we want about the company's performance. However, what about the hundreds and hundreds of small to medium enterprises throughout the industrial Midwest that virtually folded overnight because of the problems in the auto industry? We're talking about parts suppliers, small machine shops, consulting firms, recruiting firms, and dozens of other types of companies that built the automobile manufacturing industry in as their primary (or in some cases) only form of revenue. No diversification. No chance to maintain wealth once the goose stopped laying the golden eggs.

The eggs they have left were all in the same basket. Because sufficient wealth weren't accumulated, these businesses lacked the means to weather the storm. The peripheral suppliers and service providers in the automotive industry went bankrupt as well because their business model relied solely on revenue creation rather than wealth accumulation. The sudden decreases in revenue combined with the deficiency in wealth were enough to sink them.

Strategy:

Wealth planning should be the central priority for the Top Manager. Every management meeting should begin and end with this concept in mind. Furthermore, a report with a set of recommendations should be produced periodically to assess the wealth status of the organization. If you are not accumulating every week and every month of the year, then any mild storm may seriously compromise your foundation if not putting it into multiple and useless debris.

3.2. SYSTEMS & CONTROLS

Business magic is simply about formulas.

As seen in the blueprint above, the second most critical components of an organization are its **Systems and Controls**. Every business unit in the organization requires a specific system and control in order to become fully efficient. For you to master this concept, we will create a detailed set of systems and controls for the Marketing Department for COMPANY SUPERTOP. EVERY DEPARTMENT NEEDS TO HAVE ITS OWN SYSTEMS AND CONTROLS. Once you go through this model, you will have a much clearer perception as to the steps involved in creating a coherent set of systems and controls for all of the units in an organization.

Notice that at the end of every system, there will be a control to ensure that the system is implemented properly. Remember, the controls are designed to prevent staff members from engaging in **unauthorized behaviors**. If they were to try deviate from the systems' requirements, the controls would act as firewalls.

Remember:

Only the implementation of efficient systems and controls can allow the Top Manager to focus only on: Planning, Vision, Direction, and Wealth Building. YOUR ORGANIZATION NEEDS YOU TO STAY WHERE YOU BELONG. Without these systems and controls, you will remain in the business of constantly putting fires out.

Example:

To develop a complete set of systems and controls, we will assume that COMPANY SUPERTOP sells large specialized machinery to manufacturing companies. The following marketing system and controls outline the specific steps the marketing staff will apply to generate leads and sell the products for COMPANY SUPERTOP. To make it more interesting, we are also assuming that COMPANY SUPERTOP operates in a highly competitive industry with many similar businesses offering the same products—thus offering an above average customer service is critical in order to remain viable.

Here it is:

SYSTEMS AND CONTROLS – MARKETING SYSTEM

These systems and controls outline the steps we must follow to engage prospective clients and the business process requirements to sell our products.

1. **INITIAL CONTACT – QUALIFY THE LEAD**
   a. Discuss no specific details
   b. Broad Strokes, conceptual discussion
   c. Schedule Meeting
2. **OPERATIONS ANALYSIS**
   a. Client screening process
   b. Licensing
3. **PRESENT PRODUCTS BASED ON ANALYSIS**
   a. Physical Office
   b. Computer Software/Hardware
   c. Human Capital
   d. Sequential Milestones
4. **CLIENT AGREES TO MOVE FORWARD**
   a. Present Payment Structure
   b. Execution of Contract
5. **DELIVERY PROCESS**
   a. When the delivery process starts
   b. Involve clear-cut objectives
6. **FOLLOW-UP VIA CLIENT SERVICES**
   a. Marketing/Sales opportunity
   b. Keep as a client – no prospecting costs
   c. Address problems to maintain superior service

3.2.1. INITIAL CONTACT – QUALIFY THE LEAD:

- Discuss nothing specific over phone—brief exchange
- Broad strokes, conceptual discussion of products' benefits
- Schedule Meeting for Operations Analysis (on client's location)

First, "qualified leads" are those potential customers who have expressed interest in our products (whether they initiate contact with us or have been referred by our business development staff), and ostensibly meet general buying requirements (i.e., licensed to operate machineries). Upon initial contact with a qualified lead, it is the rule not to discuss our products in specific details. We will make it a point to avoid divulging exact pricing, machine specs and capabilities, delivery timeframes, and so on. We save this for further interactions.

At this point, we will be focusing on the broad capabilities of the products, and the benefits they will bring to the client. The main purpose of this exchange will be to nurture interest with the prospective client, with attention paid to avoiding any sales-pitch dialogue or needy hard-sell tactics.

Alert:

A specific set of talking points needs to be prepared prior to the initial contact exchange with the client. These talking points will emphasize the client's industry, products, challenges, as well as opportunities.

Once the client expresses the desire to learn more about our product, we will schedule an Operations Analysis on the client's location. For the industry we sell, this is a necessity in order to provide the ultimate level of service for the client. Ideally, this should be set with little delay; prompt response will not only demonstrate efficiency, but also allow us to strike while the iron is hot.

***First face-to-face meeting: 2 – 5 business days, both parties' schedules permitting.

CONTROL:

The Marketing Associate must submit the set of "talking points" for review to the Sales Manager prior to meeting any client. If the talking points are not submitted, the marketing associate is in clear violation of our policy and will no longer engage in prospecting and engaging new clients.

Once the initial meeting with the client is complete, the Marketing Associate shall submit to the Sales Manager the Plan Of Action (POA) outlining the following:

- Overview of client – General observation
- Client's Expertise in regards to products
- Client's interest level for our products
- Expected timeframe to deliver product
- Date of scheduled Operations Analysis

3.2.2. OPERATIONS ANALYSIS:

The Operations Analysis will take place subsequent to the Initial Contact. During this step of the process, we outline exactly WHAT the client needs, and what CHANGES will be required in order to align operational processes with the desired objectives.

A critical part of the Operations Analysis should address the business volume the client expects to generate in the near-term, but should also incorporate scalability factor in the long-term.

Proof of Funds:

Availability of funds to purchase our products (Will they require a loan or do they have the necessary cash on hand?)

Licensing and Permits:

Ultimately, we seek to provide products of the utmost value and quality, and therefore should expect the same attributes to be present in those to whom we provide our products. Our goal should be to ensure the highest probability of success for our clients. It is crucial in fostering a positive business reputation. The industry and business community will see a clear manifestation of our efforts and influence. This is visible in terms of the success of our clients. This is how we generate goodwill and word of mouth referrals.

Verifying that prospective clients are properly licensed is the initial step in deciding whether to pursue a business relationship. Remember, our success depends on that of our clientele ... and vice versa. Upon commencement of any project with a particular client, it is important to establish that they can in fact use the products we sell.

Exclusivity serves a purpose. It's called *"branding"*, and it's not just for the sake of inciting an artificial demand. In some instances, there is a possibility that we WILL in fact lose revenues by not selling our products to unlicensed clients. However, our long-term sustainability depends on our integrity and honesty. We do not want our clients to be faced with road barriers or penalties because they used the products we sold to them. Ultimately, the welfare and success of our clients is a major priority.

Furthermore, we will independently verify their licensure before offering our products. Some clients, albeit with the best of intentions, may be inclined to present themselves as satisfying the necessary criteria when this is in fact not the case.

**If necessary, we will assist our clients in acquiring the proper licenses and permits to operate our products. We will help them complete the application requirements. This is a value added opportunities that will help us solidify our position of superiority in comparison to our competitors.

OTHER REQUIREMENTS

Physical Office Requirement:

First, our clients will need to have a physical location from which to use our products. This space needs to be sufficient to accommodate the basic products' requirements.

Computer Systems:

As part of this analysis of the client's operations, we should evaluate their computer systems to ensure that they will accommodate their business volume and will have the capability to run the necessary software. We will also make recommendations as to the software needed to complete the job. This is another value-added service we provide to our clients; although it is not the core function of our offerings, it is a critical component and will not be neglected.

Human Capital:

In this analysis, we will determine the technical expertise of the staff members who will be operating the products. Once this analysis is complete, we will grade their staff members from 1 to 10.

CONTROL:

Proof of Funds:

Once the needs Analysis is complete, the Marketing Associate must submit a verifiable proof of income to the Sales Manager. We accept a bank statement and/or a Letter of Credit establishing that the client has the funds required to pay for our products. This is required because we cannot afford to engage in a long and resourceful implementation process without the assurance that they possess the necessary purchasing power.

Licenses and Permits:

The Sales Manager will check independently the licenses and permits of client to give Marketing Associate the green light to pursue the current relationship with the client.

Other Requirements:

The Marketing Associate must also submit the following to the Sales Manager:

- Physical Office overview
- Computer Software/Hardware overview
- Human capital grade sheet
- Custom Tailored" Application of our Products in client's operations

**If any of the items listed above do not meet the established requirements, the Marketing Associate cannot schedule the sales meeting to present products to the client. At this point, the Sales Manager retains the discretion to establish the next course of action for the Marketing Associate and client.

3.2.3. SALES MEETING – PRESENT PRODUCTS BASED ON OPERATIONAL ANALYSIS

The Presentation:

Once the Operations Analysis is complete along with the verification of the basic requirements, the Marketing Associate is given the green light the present the client with a customized approach regarding our products and operational benefits.

The strategy here is not to engage in high sales pitching but to present simply the client with a tailored application of our products within their operational requirements.

During this Sales Meeting, the objective is to demonstrate the benefits of using our products within their operations. If the client is unsure, schedule a follow-up meeting within 14 days. Under no circumstances, should the Marketing Associate engage in high-pressure sales tactics.

CONTROL:

Once the Sales meeting is complete, the Marketing Associate will submit to the Sales Manager the Sequential list of implementation objectives/project milestones.

3.2.4. CLIENT AGREES TO MOVE FORWARD:

Pricing:

The pricing of the products needs to be well articulated and explained thoroughly. This is a crucial aspect to being able to effectively market ourselves to clients, and subsequently maintain the effective progress of any particular project. We will bill 50% of the total invoice prior to beginning any work. This serves four purposes:

- It ensures that we are dealing with a client who is serious, and instills a commitment to using our products as swiftly as possible so to generate a return on investment.
- It serves to make collectability of fees more certain as the project draws to a close, since the client has already laid out significant resources and will therefore be committed to completing the cycle. It also protects us in the event that the client becomes insolvent.
- Included in the predetermined pricing of products communicated to the client, we will outline the future payments schedule with established milestones in the implementation of the model. It also assists us in creating an organized delivery system to keep everyone on track.
- Because payments are attached to milestones, the outlay of the initial lump-sum retainer needs to be associated with a significant portion of our service provisions/deliverables. Therefore, rapid implementation of our products within their operations is important, not only for a fast turnaround, but also in demonstrating to the client that a large portion of the work is quickly completed.

**Issues with pricing:

Question:

What if the client rejects the pricing structure?

Answer:

We do not cut prices or negotiate. Additionally, we do not offer a watered-down version of our products, as this could hurt perception of quality. It is all or nothing.

The client accepts the PRICING:

At this point, we can execute the contract and we are to begin the implementation process immediately.

CONTROL:

The Sales Management must verify that the first payment has been made before giving the green light to initiate the delivery and implementation process.

3.2.5. DELIVERY PROCESS:

The Delivery Process should begin immediately after a contract has been executed. While the start time will depend on a variety of factors (scheduling on both sides), it is important for progress to be shown as soon as possible.

The Sales Manager must develop clear-cut order of project milestones as part of the implementation cycle, but whenever possible should refrain from setting or committing to a rigid timeline. Failure to meet precisely established objectives on an overly ambitious schedule can cause dissatisfaction/apprehension with the client, despite the level of positive progress.

CONTROL:

Prior to the Delivery Process, an internal meeting between the marketing staff and operations staff needs to be scheduled to discuss the implementation plan. This meeting is critical and mandatory because it will prevent us from becoming overbooked and incapable of meeting our contractual agreements.

3.2.6. FOLLOW-UP & CUSTOMER SERVICES:

Although we anticipate the implementation phase to be smooth and well executed, we should expect the client to engage us in an ongoing base for troubleshooting and general questions and answers. This is when our Customer Service Department takes over to serve the client's needs.

Customer Service Department – Ongoing Consulting Support:

- Cater to existing clients
- Generates indirect income

Once we have the client up and running with our products, we will conduct ongoing bi-annual follow-up reviews to ensure our products are operating smoothly. This also affords us the opportunity to evaluate clients' needs for additional products and services we could offer.

While this branch of our operations generates no direct income, their role is to maintain and nurture the business relationship with clients who are already familiar with (and presumably satisfied with) our products.

During follow-up reviews, potential problem areas need to be addressed. This serves two purposes:

- It ensures complete satisfaction with our products
- It allows us to identify and determine possibilities for the provision of future products

By monitoring progress, we are also able to remain in contact with the client and manage the business relationship with a focus on longevity and customer satisfaction.

CONTROL:

The Customer Service Manager has to submit to the Operations Manager a bi-monthly report of all current and past clients. This report will outline the following:

- Satisfaction level with products
- Areas of concerns and solutions offered
- Possibility of future sales

THAT'S IT. We just built a comprehensive set of systems and controls for the marketing department and personnel. It establishes the process of operation at each critical step for this department. Everyone knows in detail what to do and what to avoid. It also outlines the clear lines of accountability. Essentially, no employees can operate beyond their box. If there is a problem along the process, then it will be easy to spot where and who "dropped the ball" As you can tell, the systems controls were also written as if it was a **training manual.** It explains to the employees why certain rules exist and how it helps to organization promote broad efficiency and a lasting brand.

3.3. STAFFING:

Every finished puzzle is admirable.

The primary goal when building a team should be to instill consistency and to promote excellence when assigned tasks are executed. The model outlined below is very innovative and there is nothing else in concept or in practice available to match its efficacy. In fact, the best consultants in the world use it to turn dysfunctional employees into stellar performers. With this expertise, you will set yourself apart from the usual manager who uses feeble management tools.

This model emphasizes the necessity to achieve the two following standards:

- Complete understanding of assigned responsibilities
- Optimum execution at all times

To meet the two standards above, you will need to develop the following progressive Package for every employee:

1. Job requirements/descriptions/duties—It is all the same.
2. Quantifiable Performance Metrics
3. Evaluation System
4. Adjustment System
5. Incentive System
6. Skill Enhancement System

To remain consistent, we will create the Package for a Marketing Associate since the systems and controls for the marketing department are complete. The goal of this package is to integrate the Marketing Associate into the overall Marketing System of the organization. After each item in the package, there will be a "Debrief" section to explain what has been accomplished. You should keep in mind that this is an internal package and it is assuming that the Marketing Associate has already been hired. The Marketing Associate has to sign this document so to emphasize the fact that it is a contractual agreement between he/she and the company and all of its components are well understood.

Note:

The sections about educational requirements, experience, etc. do not belong in this package because this is not a job advertisement.

Here it is:

MARKETING ASSOCIATE:

Overview:

The Marketing Associate (MA) is part of the Marketing Department and reports directly to the Sales Manager.

3.3.1. JOB REQUIREMENTS:

The MA is responsible for the following duties:

- Generate Leads
- Qualify Leads
- Close Leads

Debrief:

As you can tell, the job requirements are very simple and straight to the point. Ideally, you should not use more than ten words for every requirement. If a job requirement requires paragraphs after paragraphs of explanation, then consider it inefficient. In this section, the primary goal is to avoid confusion.

3.3.2. QUANTIFIABLE PERFORMANCE METRICS:

The MA will be evaluated monthly based on the following metrics:

Generation of leads:

THE MA MUST GENERATE 100 LEADS PER MONTH.

**The leads will come from face-to-face marketing, online, and "direct cold calls'" referrals.

Qualifying Leads:

THE MA MUST QUALIFY 50 LEADS PER MONTH.

**A lead is considered qualified if it meets the basic requirements as outlined in the Marketing system.

The basic requirements for a qualified lead are as follow:

1. The lead has the financial ability to purchase our products
2. The lead has the space available to use our products within their facility
3. The lead has the staff and technical expertise to operate our products

Closing The Leads:

THE MA MUST CLOSE 10 LEADS PER MONTH.

**A lead is considered "closed" if a contract has been executed with a customer and 50% of the total billable fee has been received.

Debrief:

For every job requirement, there should be a quantifiable metric to track success or failure. In essence, there is a minimum standard to meet for every job duty. If this standard is not met, then the manager has the mathematical evidence to base any decision whether it is to reassign or terminate an employee. This is the reason why it is essential to have the employee sign this document before they start. With this contract, an employee can never contest the foundation and fairness of a managerial decision.

Dilemma:

In some instances, it could be difficult to develop quantifiable metrics for a "qualitative employee". For instance, the receptionist who only answers the phone performs "qualitative work". When faced with this situation, you have to assign that "qualitative employee" to a specific department that uses quantifiable metrics.

Possible solution:

We could possibly assign the receptionist to the customer service department. In the most successful organizations, one of the metrics used to evaluate the customer service departments is by the number of consumer complaints they receive every month. Usually their acceptable standard is a specific number—for example 30. Accordingly, if the complaints were to exceed 30, then the entire department including the receptionist will receive a failing grade.

Bottom Line:

All employees can be evaluated with quantifiable metrics regardless of the qualitative work they may perform. If not directly possibly, the basic strategy is to determine which department possessing quantifiable metrics closely matches their job duties.

3.3.3. EVALUATION SYSTEM:

GENERATION OF LEADS:

- Success Grade : 90 % or more (90% X 100) = 90 or more
- Failure Grade : 89% or less (89 % X 100) = 89 or less

QUALIFYING LEADS:

- Success Grade: 90 % or more (90% X 50) = 45 or more
- Failure Grade : 89% or less (89% X 50) = ~ 44 or less*

CLOSING THE LEADS:

- Success Grade: 90 % or more (90% X 10) = 9 or more
- Failure Grade: 89% or less (89% X 10) = ~ 8 or less*

*We are rounding down because a customer is whole.

Debrief:

The success and failure grades may vary based on the company and industry, the type of product or service, and competitive forces. However, your minimum standard should always be at 90 % and up. If it is hard to implement this standard, then some type of inefficiency within your system itself may exist.

3.3.4. ADJUSTMENT PLAN:

Priority Plan:

If the Marketing Associate does not meet the required monthly success grade in any of the following: Generation of Leads, Qualifying Leads, and Closings Leads, then the priority plan will automatically go in effect.

At the discretion of the Sales Manager, it will include at least four of the following:

- Geographical reassignment
- Sales retraining
- Skills and expertise reevaluation (The employee's assessment developed earlier can be used for this purpose)
- Contract execution support
- Shadow Marketing Associates with "passing grades"

Plan for Success and Failure:

Once the priority plan is complete, the Marketing Associate has one calendar month to meet the success grades as outlined above.

If the standard is still not met at the end of the calendar month, the Sales Manager will only have two options to choose from:

- Transfer the Marketing Associate to another department
- Terminate effectively the Marketing Associate

Debrief:

As you can tell for the Plan for Success and Failure, it is clear and specific. The options do not overlap each other and are easy to understand from an employee's perspective.

Insight:

It is always easier to retrain ineffective employees rather than hire new ones. Many studies show that companies use a great deal of resources (human and capital) to advertise, interview, hire, and train new employees. For this reason, a revolving door policy is never the best approach.

3.3.5. INCENTIVE SYSTEM:

If the Marketing Associate meets the success standards for 12 consecutive months, then a 30% bonus will be added to his/her total base salary established in the job offer letter.

BONUS FORMULA = (BASE SALARY * 30%)

*There will be no bonus allocation if the Marketing Associate does not meet the success standards for 12 consecutive months.

Debrief:

As you can tell, this is a very simple incentive program. The formulas for any incentive programs whether it is a bonus, vacation, or a new car must be clear, concise, and undisputable. If you cannot create an incentive program following these basic principles, then you should not put it into effect.

Insight:

Spending accounts are a very good example for tricky incentive programs. Their methods of disbursements are always confusing and difficult to convey to employees.

3.3.6. SKILL ENHANCEMENT SYSTEM:

The MA has to take part in the following:

- Attend weekly sales meeting with the Sales managers and other Marketing Associates
- Attend monthly Sales Training
- Attend monthly debriefs with Marketing Team
- Complete at least 3 semester credit hours in marketing management per year
- Participate in yearly seminars and online training programs scheduled by the company

***Every authorized training program will be reimbursed to the employee.*

Debrief:

The skill enhancement system should revolve around the employee's job duties. In essence, for every job duty, there should be a training program in place. In this case, the skill enhancement systems outlined above should help an employee excel in generating, qualifying, and closing leads.

Employee Signature <u>Patrick Morris</u>

Sales Manager Signature: <u>Brenda Smith</u>

WE ARE DONE! We have just completed the most efficient and comprehensive package for an employee in an organization. It includes all of the elements required to promote success, growth, and organizational effectiveness. Again, each employee in the organization must have this type of package developed on their behalf before their first day of work.

3.4. RETURN ON INVESTMENT (ROI):

Without good returns, you don't have anything to show.

We have already covered the ROI in the Business Analysis section under the Comparative Cost Analysis (CCA). As stated, the CCA is the tool used to determine the best ROI for each cost structure in an organization. Once this analysis is complete, the best ROI becomes the standard moving forward.

Example:

Let's assume that it is the beginning of Year 2009 and we want to establish the ROI standard for the Marketing Department for the rest of the year. Accordingly, we have compiled the financial data for the past 4 years for COMPANY SUPERTOP.

A. Total Sales:

Description	2005	2006	2007	2008
Sales	$3,000,000	$8,700,000	$7,000,000	$4,500,000

B. Total Marketing Cost:

Description	2005	2006	2007	2008
Marketing Salaries	$400,000	$900,000	$800,000	$500,000
Marketing Cost	$120,000	$570,000	$425,000	$230,000
Total Cost	**$520,000**	**$1,470,000**	**$1,225,000**	**$730,000**

* Marketing Cost includes print, media, TV, radio, supplies, etc .

C. ROI Calculation:

Description	2005	2006	2007	2008
Sales	$3,000,000	$8,700,000	$7,000,000	$4,500,000
Total Cost	$520,000	$1,470,000	$1,225,000	$730,000
ROIs (Sales ÷ TC)	$5.77	$5.92	$5.71	$6.16

Debrief:

As seen above, the best ROI is $6.16. This means that moving forward; $6.16 is the standard to meet at a minimum for all of the subsequent weeks, months, and years starting in 2009.

3.5. CONTINGENCY PLAN:

Everyone will smack at a wall once a while.

The Contingency Plan represents the options available to a company if its ROI drops in regards to the established standard. In other words, it is the "get back on track" system. In this case, $6.16 is established ROI the Marketing Department must sustain at least for every upcoming week, month, quarter, and year of operation starting in 2009.

Note:

It is expected for this standard to remain attainable because the Marketing Department has already proven that this milestone is a possibility.

Example:

What if the standard ROI drops by 20%?

Multiple avenues can force the standard ROI to drop by 20%. Here are just a few:

- Sales decreases
- Marketing Cost increases
- Sales decreases and Marketing Cost increases simultaneously

Review:

The standard ROI was achieved in 2008 from the following calculation:

Description	2008
Marketing Salaries	$500,000
Marketing Costs	$230,000
Total Costs (TC)	**$730,000**
Sales	$4,500,000
ROIs (Sales/TC)	**$6.16**

Possible Scenarios:

Scenario 1: Sales decrease

Here, we have to find by how much the decrease in Sales has caused the ROI to drop by 20% (= $6.16 – 20% = $4.93)

Hint:

Microsoft Excel Solver is a great tool available to perform these types of simulations.

Holding everything else constant, a drop in Sales from $4,500,000 to $3,598,900 will cause the ROI to fall to $4.93 as seen below:

Description	2009
Marketing Salaries	$500,000
Marketing Costs	$230,000
Total Cost (TC)	**$730,000**
Sales	**$3,598,900**
ROIs (Sales/TC)	**$4.93**

Scenario 2: Marketing Cost increases:

Description	2009
Marketing Salaries	$591,389
Marketing Cost	$321,390
Total Cost (TC)	**$912,779**
Sales	**$4,500,000**
ROIs (Sales/TC)	**$4.93**

Scenario 3: Sales decrease and Marketing Cost increases simultaneously:

Description	2009
Marketing Salaries	$589,910
Marketing Cost	$319,910
Total Costs (TC)	**$909,821**
Sales	**$4,485,415**
ROIs (Sales/TC)	**$4.93**

The Contingency Plan:

Let's assume this scenario when Sales decrease and the Marketing Cost increases.

Description	2009
Marketing Salaries	$589,910
Marketing Cost	$319,910
Total Costs (TC)	**$909,821**
Sales	**$4,485,415**
ROIs (Sales/TC)	**$4.93**

Question:

How do we return to the established ROI, which is $6.16?

There are three routes available; and they should be taken in the following order:

First and best Option: Cut Costs:

Cutting cost is the first route you should always take to return to the best ROI. Fundamentally, it is the easiest to accomplish because it is an internal matter and all of the variables can be controlled by the manager.

Major insight: to reach the desired level of profitability/return on investment, it is always easier to cut cost than increase revenues.

Question:

By how much the Marketing Cost needs to decrease to return the ROI back to $6.16.

Reminder: The current Marketing Cost is: $319,910.

Again, Microsoft Excel Solver will ease this computation.

Answer:

Description	2010
Marketing Salaries	$589,910
Marketing Cost	**$138,241**
Total Costs (TC)	**$728,152**
Sales	$4,485,415
ROIs (Sales/TC)	**$6.16**

As you can tell above, the Marketing Cost needs to decrease from $319,910 to $138,241 for the ROI to return to $6.16. Or, decrease by $181,669.

Here is the process you should use to reduce the Marketing Cost for example:

1. First, itemize each cost line by line

2. Second, eliminate every cost lacking a quantifiable metric system to measure its EFFICACY.

3. Third, eliminate other costs that will not hinder short-term business continuity

Second option: Increase Sales:

This option will always be harder than the first one because it includes the external environment. As you may suspect, most businesses operate in a competitive environment where price wars and are the norms. For this reason, acquiring many new customers in a short period can be difficult if the market is saturated with competitors. However, an aggressive and smart marketing strategy should increase Sales.

Question:

By how much Sales need to increase to return the ROI back to $6.16?

Answer:

Description	2010
Marketing Salaries	$589,910
Marketing Cost	$319,910
Total Cost (TC)	**$909,821**
Sales	**$5,604,494**
ROIs (Sales/TC)	**$6.16**

As you can tell, Sales need to increase from $4,485,415 to $5,604,494 for the ROI to return to $6.16. Or, increase by $1,119,080.

You should use the following strategy:

First, perform an analysis of the past marketing strategies you have utilized and establish which ones yielded the highest returns

Second, identify the opportunities available within the market and determine if the organization is operationally suited to pursue them

Third, determine the exact additional income required to reach the established ROI.

Wow Factor:

As seen in the two scenarios above, for the ROI to return to $6.16, COMPANY SUPERTOP must either reduce Marketing Cost by $181,669 or increase Sales by $1,119,080.

Question:

Which option is easier to achieve?

Answer:

Of course, reduce Marketing Cost.

Fact:

It is always easier to reduce cost than increase Sales to reach the best ROI. In this example, the additional income needed to attain the standard ROI amounts to approximately six times the required cost reduction amount ($1,119,080 vs. $181,669)

Insight:

Many small to mid-sized businesses believe that all of their financial problems will be solved if only they generated more sales. The example above demonstrates that this belief is a pure myth.

Third option: Cut Salaries or terminate employees:

If reducing cost and increasing sales are not possible, then a company must resort to its last option: Cutting salaries or terminating employees.

Cutting salaries or terminating employees should be the last option because of the following main reasons:

1. Cutting salaries will deplete the employees' morale
2. Terminating employees sends the signal of a failing company
3. In some case, a whole community may be affected if the layoffs are substantial

Example:

Let's assume that COMPANY SUPERTOP employs ten employees in the marketing department and they each earn $58,991 a year. This amounts to $589,910 a year.

First option: Reduce Salaries
Answer:

Description	2010
Marketing Salaries	**$408,241**
Marketing Cost	$319,910
Total Cost (TC)	**$728,152**
Sales	$4,485,415
ROIs (Sales/TC)	**$6.16**

Debrief:

Holding everything else constant, the Marketing Salaries needs to decrease from $589,910 to **$408,241** for the standard to return to $6.16. Or, decrease by $181,669.

Since there are 10 employees, each salary will need decrease by ~$18,167 ($181,669 ÷ 10). Therefore, each employee's salary will decrease from $58,991/year to $40,824/year.

Second Option: Terminate Employees:

 In some cases, it is impossible to reduce the salaries of some employees. They may have signed specific contracts, the industry may dictate a specific income, or the federal minimum wage requirement may prevent it. In cases like these, layoffs are the only option left.

Answer:

Since the excess Marketing Salaries amounts to $181,669 and each employee earns $58,991/year, the number of employees to terminate is: ~4 ($181,669 ÷ $58,167). The mathematical answer is 3.08 employees. Since each employee is considered a whole person, we have to round 3.08 to the next digit up, which is 4.

Note:

Terminating 4 employees will over-exceed the required standard ROI of $6.16 because only terminating 3.08 employees is required to attain it. If you do the calculation correctly, you will find that the ROI will jump to $6.66 and surpass the minimum required ROI of $6.16.

Insight:

Have you ever wondered how large companies base their expected layoff figures? The process above is one of the methods they use.

3.6. GOAL:

Even Einstein could have done it better.

An organization seeking to remain efficient should always establish specific goals to reach. The basic structure of this goal-setting system is to outperform consistently the current Return On Investment (ROI) for each department.

Bottom Line:

Creating a platform in which standards have to increase progressively, gives the organization the ability to prevail over its competition while securing its chances of long-term sustainability.

Process:

There are multiple means available to set ROI goals. The most popular is the percentage-based method.

Example:

As seen below, the ROI for the marketing department is currently $6.16.

Description	2008
Marketing Salaries	$500,000
Marketing Cost	$230,000
Total Cost (TC)	**$730,000**
Sales	$4,500,000
ROI (Sales/TC)	**$6.16**

Possible Goal:

COMPANY SUPERTOP can establish as goal to increase its current ROI by 10% for the upcoming year (2009)

Solution:

Holding everything else constant, the answer is $6.78 ($6.16 * 1.1)

Note:

Achieving this new goal for the year 2009 is possible through multiple routes. It could be done by reducing total marketing cost and/or increasing sales.

A. Route 1: Reduce Total Cost to achieve a ROI of $6.78

Description	2009
Marketing Salaries	**$500,000**
Marketing Cost	**$163,717**
Total Cost (TC)	**$663,717**
Sales	$4,500,000
ROIs (Sales/TC)	**$6.78**

Debrief:

Holding everything else constant, the Total Cost needs to decrease from $730,000 to $663,717 for the ROI to increase to $6.78.

B. Route 2: Increase Sales

Description	2009
Marketing Salaries	$500,000
Marketing Costs	$230,000
Total Costs (TC)	**$730,000**
Sales	**$4,949,400**
ROIs (Sales/TC)	**$6.78**

Debrief:

Holding everything else constant, Sales need to increase from $4,500,000 to $4,949,400 for the ROI to increase to $6.78.

SUMMARY:

We are done. We have just built the entire Marketing Department for COMPANY SUPERTOP. It looks like this:

TOP MANAGER'S RESPONSIBILITIES: PLANNING – VISION –DIRECTION- WEALTH BUILDING
SYSTEM: MARKETING
1. Qualify The Lead - Control 1   2. Operations Analysis - Control 2   3. Present Products Control 3   4. Client Agrees To Move Forward - Control 4   5. Delivery Process - Control 5   6. Follow-Up via Client Services - Control 6
STAFF
1. Job Requirement   2. Quantifiable Performance Metrics   3. Evaluation System   4. Incentive System   5. Skill Enhancement System
ROI
ROI Achieved in 2008   **$6.16 is the Standard Moving Forward**
CONTINGENCY PLANS
1. Reduce Cost   2. Increase Sales   3. Reduce Salaries
GOAL: 2009
10% ROI Increase   **$6.78**

This innovative model can be built for every department an organization. In the following departments for example:

- Accounting and Finance
- Purchasing
- Production
- Quality Control
- Research & Development
- Public Relations

Bottom Line:

You will create the best organizational structure if you develop this Top-Down model. It has proven itself overwhelmingly in the most successful organizations in the world. As you can tell, this model starts with the responsibilities of the Top Manager, and then we have the specific systems and controls, and all of the way down to the GOAL. It gives an organization the specific blueprint just like building a house from scratch.

SECTION IV - OPTIMIZE FOR ULTIMATE EFFICIENCY:

In SECTION 3, you learned how to build the perfect organizational structure using a proven and effective model. In this chapter, you will learn how to optimize the management systems of an organization by focusing on some critical elements that will lead to continuous efficiency. The tools we will cover in this section will enhance the decision-making process of any leader. They are quick tune-ups you can implement immediately for any organization. We will call classify these management tools as the "**11 REQUIRED NUTS AND BOLTS**" for a well-operated organization.

Here they are:

1. Install Flash Reports To Simplify Management's Decision Making Process
2. Develop Optimum Pricing Strategy And Structure
3. Separate Direct From Indirect Cost
4. Departmentalize Financial Statements By Departments And Units
5. Install Optimum Operating Budget
6. Install A Cyclical Inventory System
7. Install An Efficient Receivables Collection System
8. Develop Efficient Quality Control Standards
9. Develop Optimum Distribution Channels
10. Develop The Best Sales Strategy
11. Determine The Optimum Number Of Locations

4.1. INSTALL FLASH REPORTS:

Simplify your decision-making process and your life will get simpler.

Insight:

In many organizations, the production of any quick management report is very difficult. The creation of these reports may require a considerable amount of labor time as well as tedious number crunching. In some cases, months may go by before the real numbers are uncovered. Consequently, short-term decisions in these organizations remain flawed. For instance, the inability to develop a timely report on the status of inventory results into estimations. And as you may suspect, it is always a bad proposition to guesstimate in areas where mathematical accuracy is crucial.

Problem:

The imprecise inventory level may create for example, delivery issues, and thus, customers may never receive their products on time. Or even, it may cause the organization to hold more inventory than necessary, which may lead to the destruction, clutter, expiration, and pilferage of products.

Now assume quick management reports such as the inventory levels or the cash flow status were non-existent for managers. You could foresee the management "putting fires out" constantly because the simple tools to make good decisions are lacking. This is the reason why so many believe this notion that managing an organization is stressful when in fact it is not. It can enjoyable and exciting if the production of quick and accurate reports is a managerial priority.

Bottom Line:

As a Top Manager, you need good information to make decisions. And this information must available to you right away when the decision needs to be made. You will have to use the appropriate technologies and combine them with the implementation of a workflow process efficient enough to support the development of these reports with ease.

These reports need not to be complicated. They can be simple but must help the manager to outline quickly the next plan of action without waiting.

The term "Flash" refers to the rapidity of gathering useful Business Intelligence as frequently as on a daily basis. These reports must be readily available for review to be considered: Flash. The combination of all of the flash reports will give the management a current and precise overview of the organization's financial and operational position. Accordingly, the decision-making process becomes more absolute. The following reports must available within a flash notice:

1. Overhead And Variable Costs Allocation
2. Sales Data
3. Gross Margins
4. Cash Flow Status
5. Break-Even Position
6. Inventory Level
7. Accounts Receivable
8. Accounts Payable
9. Production/Servicing Output

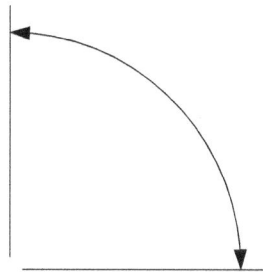

Example 1:

INVENTORY FLASH REPORT	
Date	7/1/2000
Available inventory (units)	5000
Maximum capacity (units)	10,000
Average daily turnover	500
Average weekly turnover	2,500
Expected Days to limit	10

Now, let's demonstrate how useful this simple flash report is:

1. Available inventory (5000): it represents the number of units the company has available on shelf
2. Maximum capacity (10,000): it represents the total units the company can hold on shelf
3. Average daily turnover (500): it represents the number of units sold every working day
4. Average weekly turnover (2,500): it represents the number of units sold every week

And Now...

The most important information with this flash report is the "Days to limit". **In this case, it is 10.** It tells the inventory manager that in 10 days, the company will not be able to satisfy its average sales. If it takes 15 days for example to reorder products, then of course the company will not be able to fill its orders. If the inventory level report is accurate and available every morning on the desk of the Inventory Manager, then this organization may never be unprepared. If the Inventory Manager has to go through a cumbersome process just gather this information, then his decision-making process will always be compromised. He may either over-purchase or under-purchase inventory. Both scenarios will result into a loss of profitability.

Example 2:

CURRENT GROSS MARGIN FLASH REPORT	
Date	7/1/2000
Product A	65%
Product B	12%
Product C	75%
Product D	27%
Product E	44%
Product F	55%

Now, let's demonstrate how useful this simple flash report is:

For many organizations, this type of information is only available maybe once or twice a year. Would you want to wait until the end of the year to figure out that a specific product (Product B for example) yielded only a 12% gross margin? Of course not. You want to find this information fast and take the necessary corrective action.

Here is the reason:

If you average out all of the products' gross margins including Product B, it is: **46%.** Let's assume that you found right away that Product B is yielding a disastrous gross margin and eliminated it from your offerings. Holding everything else constant, your overall gross margin would increase to **53%.** This is another reason why Flash reports are so indispensable to the daily decision-making process. **They allow you to spotlight issues fast while enabling a manager to take quick and decisive actions.**

4.2. DEVELOP OPTIMUM PRICING STRATEGY AND STRUCTURE:

Having a rock solid strategy is easier than you think.

Insight:

There are multiple pricing structures and strategies available to implement. For instance, a smaller company with hopes of integrating a larger market may engage in price penetration strategies. With this approach, a low introductory pricing tactic may be best to lure in new customers. Alternatively, a more well-known company may use the differentiation pricing strategy. In this case, the strength of its brand may warrant a premium pricing strategy without fears of losing the already acquired market share to the less established companies.

Nevertheless, the majority of organizations use Cost-Plus Pricing, which simply adds a mark-up on top of the cost of production/servicing. The goal of this simple pricing strategy is to earn a profit from operating a business. The only problem with a Cost-Plus Pricing strategy lies in the realm of long-term feasibility. For example, earning a 1% in profits may accomplish the general expected goal but may not result in long-term sustainability. In other words, wealth accumulation will not become reality.

Solution:

We will propose the concept of "Minimum Acceptable Profit (MAP)" regardless of the pricing strategy. The MAP is the established and exact threshold of profitability a company must attain to warrant its existence. In terms of operating a successful business, it should be unacceptable to engage in any pricing method that does not provide a MAP. If for example the expected MAP is 20% of sales, then the pricing structure must reflect this objective. Here the strategy is to **use the MAP as cost center**. Just like paying for the mortgage/lease or the electric bill, the company will classify this MAP as the most important cost above anything else. This

MAP should be the first cost a company must pay above anything else. The approach is the only route that will guarantee constant profitability.

Example:

Let's assume that COMPANY SUPERTOP's Minimum Acceptable Profit (MAP) is 20% of Sales.

Here is the simple Solution:

Sales	$1,000,000
COGS	$300,000
Gross Margin	**$700,000**
Variable Costs	$150,000
Fixed Costs	$200,000
Earnings Before Tax	**$350,000**
Tax (30%)	$105,000
MAP (20% Of Sales)	**$200,000**
Net Profit	$45,000

Debrief:

As you can tell, the MAP is structured as a cost to be paid out to the company itself. With this model, COMPANY SUPERTOP's Net Profit becomes essentially the bonus because it is what's left after the MAP has been secured. The leaders in the most successful organizations will place this entire MAP into the company's "Wealth Box" (Savings Accounts). This gives them the assurance that they can withstand future contingencies.

They may use the Net Profit to give out annual bonuses to employees, invest in Research & Development or whatever else they want.

Big Question:

What happens if after paying for the MAP, there isn't enough left to cover the rest of the costs?

Answer:

The Company needs to change its overall business model because failing consistently to secure the MAP leaves it vulnerable to future uncertainties. If a company must lower its established MAP standard to pay for other costs, then its chances of long-term survival will be slim. Just paying bills and managing to stay above water is a losing strategy to begin with.

Insight:

Again, the lack of accumulated wealth is one of the main reasons why the majority of new businesses fail within 5 years of operation. These businesses can never build enough prosperity to sustain economic downturns and market shifts.

The ultimate benchmark is to always the MAP for any effective pricing strategy. Once the MAP is reached, then any other pricing strategies may be acceptable as market situations evolve.

4.3. SEPARATE DIRECT COST FROM INDIRECT COST:

The cooperation between Water and Sand is why we love the beach.

Many organizations use erroneous formulas or the wrong approaches when classifying which costs are direct and which are indirect (overhead/fixed). This creates a significant managerial problem because the results derived from any financial analysis are usually flawed and ultimately, lead to bad decisions.

Example:

The cost of travel in many organizations is classified as overhead when in reality they are direct costs. If a Marketing Associate travels across state to sell a company's products, then the travel cost should be considered as a selling cost, which is a direct cost. Therefore, the cost of travel should be included in the Cost of Goods Sold column in order to establish the total cost of the products. This little mistake leads many organizations to conclude that the Total Cost of their products is cheaper than in reality. As a result, any Cost-Plus Pricing structure will be flawed because they will be based on the wrong foundation.

Insight:

The wrong allocation of overhead cost may also lead to the wrong staff makeup. For example, a manager may determine that the overhead percentage is too high and non-sustainable because there are too many employees on salaries. With this conclusion, this manager may terminate many necessary employees by wrongly classifying staff members—Instead of Direct Labor, they will be in the salaried column.

Solution:

In order to separate effectively the direct cost from overhead, you must follow the following two rules:

Rule 1: Direct Costs are easy to calculate:

If you have trouble allocating a cost to a specific unit in the organization, then it is probably an overhead cost. Overhead Costs usually span over months and may come from many directions. Direct Costs are easy to identify. They usually include direct materials and direct labor cost. When outlining Direct Costs, complex financial computations or complex allocation processes aren't necessary.

Rule 2: Overhead Costs are non-negotiable:

Overhead costs are non-negotiable because they serve as the lifeline of the business. Without them, the business cannot survive. If you could eliminate a cost, then it is probably a direct cost. An organization may not survive without incurring the cost of rent and utilities for example. Overhead cost affects the immediate survival of a business. Other cost such as office supplies are in the grey area. Even though they are not directly attributable to the direct production of a product, they still constitute an essential part in the delivery of products and services. Some managers will split and allocate the cost half-and-half between direct and indirect to satisfy this ambiguity. Whichever is the strategy, it must be established with only two non-negotiable choices: survival vs. non-survival. Or, Overhead Cost vs. Direct Cost.

4.4. DEPARTMENTALIZE FINANCIAL STATEMENTS:

With smart break-downs, everyone's job is easier.

Insight:

Many organizations struggle to gather and process their financial information because they utilize only one system to process every transaction.

The following flawed system represents for example, the usual process utilized by the accounting department in many organizations:

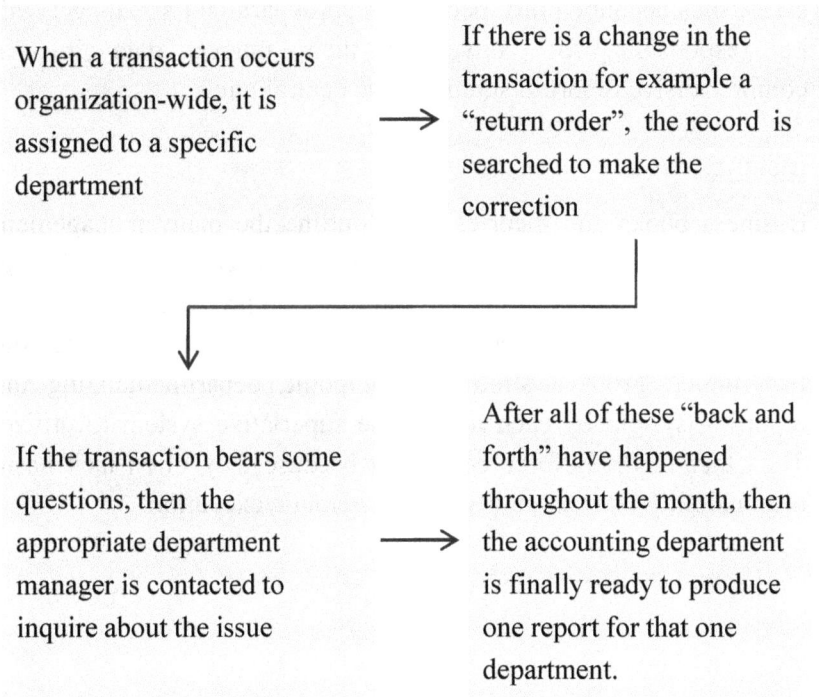

When a transaction occurs organization-wide, it is assigned to a specific department

$\longrightarrow$

If there is a change in the transaction for example a "return order", the record is searched to make the correction

If the transaction bears some questions, then the appropriate department manager is contacted to inquire about the issue

$\longrightarrow$

After all of these "back and forth" have happened throughout the month, then the accounting department is finally ready to produce one report for that one department.

Now, The Accounting Department must repeat each of the four processes for each department. Without doubt, this is an inefficient and time-consuming process that to leads frustration, endless repetitions, and errors.

Solution:

The first three processes could be easily avoided by simply requiring each department to be in charge of their own transactions. They can fix/update financial transactions that apply specifically to their department much more easily and rapidly than a central accounting department.

The proposed strategy here is to create an assembly line of processing information through each department leading to one comprehensive package. In terms of management efficiency, it establishes accountability because each department's manager will be responsible for converting their unique data into a comprehensive report to submit to the central unit.

Insight:

Business books and theories often outline the many management systems available to implement within an organizational setting. Furthermore, these books often point out the pros/cons when using various management reporting systems without declaring the frontrunner. From a strategic standpoint, departmentalizing the reporting system by each unit is the superlative system to utilize. The other methods force confusion because they often lack basic responsibility, accountability, and systematic execution.

4.5. INSTALL OPTIMUM OPERATING BUDGET:

Save money for the storm and you will have a shelter.

Every organization needs to develop an efficient budgeting system to forecast how much is necessary to cover operational costs, prepare for future contingencies, and earn the established Minimum Acceptable Profit (MAP). Once this final budget amount is established, then it will become the goal for the marketing department to generate in sales.

The following budgeting model is innovative and effective. It includes the following four components:

- The Known-Knowns (KKs)
- The Known-Unknowns (KUs)
- The Unknown-Unknowns (UUs)
- MAP assignment

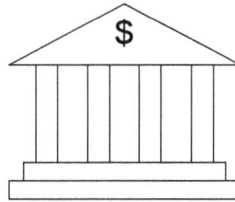

4.5.1. THE KNOWN-KNOWNS (KKS):

The KKs are those costs an organization will incur regardless of volume or future market changes. These costs are certain. Generally, they include overhead costs such as the lease/mortgage, building maintenance, utilities, signed contracts, insurance, office salaries, taxes, etc.

Note:

The KKs may vary based on each organization's specific structure and industry.

Assume that the following costs are the established KKs for COMPANY SUPERTOP in 2011:

Lease	$120,000
Insurance	$35,000
Taxes	$340,000
Contracts	$245,000
Utilities	$27,000
Office Salaries	$920,000
Office Supplies	$22,000
Budget for KKs	**$1,709,000**

Debrief:

Regardless of business volume, COMPANY SUPERTOP will incur $1,709,000 in KKs in 2011.

4.5.2. THE KNOWN-UNKNOWNS (KUS):

The KUs are those costs an organization projects to incur if some situations were to evolve. Essentially, preparing for the KUs is like formulating a backup or contingency plan. Think about it like being a responsible homeowner that sets money aside each year for inevitable repair and maintenance expenditures that he might encounter over the years; like replacing a roof, a hot water heater, or an air conditioning unit. All can be major expenditures, but can also be quite bearable if taken into account before the emergency arose. So how do we choose what potential elements to include in the KU category when devising this budget line item?

The best strategy to generate KUs is to assign a probability for every possible scenario. This is when a management team's experience and expertise comes handy. For example, let's assume that COMPANY SUPERTOP is in the transportation industry. The company has a fleet of 20 different trucks to deliver the products of its clients. And the acquisition price for each truck is $100,000 for example.

But business has volume has been high lately. The Company has been sending trucks all across the country the past several months. Because expansion has been more rapid than anticipated, many of these trucks are putting on double the mileage than originally expected. Let's assume that because of the extra mileage and more frequent use that 10 of these trucks have been in and out of the mechanic shop for repairs. This should be expected since the 20-truck fleet is doing the job of 25+ trucks. There's been a lot of overtime on the engines, and this level of usage was not called for in the original operating plan or budget.

It would be foolish for the management team NOT to budget for the possibility of purchasing 10 new trucks for the upcoming year. Many of the trucks in the fleet are having problems. However, there is the possibility that the 10 problematic trucks will perform satisfactorily in the following year given the proper maintenance. Perhaps not EVERY truck will require replacement. Consequently, to budget the TOTAL amount required to purchase 10 new trucks is impractical. There is still a lot of uncertainty surrounding how many trucks will be needed. Perhaps the Company would be able to sufficiently meet the demands of business volume and encounter few additional mechanical problems by only purchasing half of that number. There is a distinct uncertainty factor. This is the reason why KUs are budgeted using a *probability system*.

For example, the management team may decide that there is 20% chance that all 10 trucks will have to be replaced. This decision could have been based on past experiences or from another analysis process.

Here is the Solution:

Price of each new truck	$100,000
Number of unreliable trucks	10
Total cost if all 10 trucks are replaced	$1,000,000
Probability of occurrence	20%
Budget for KUs for Trucks	**$200,000**

To complete this budget section, the process shown above must be repeated for every cost the organization foresees as a KU.

Let's assume that following are also the areas of concerns for the management team:

- Computer System: Total Cost: $35,000 – Probability: 30%
- Building Repairs: Total Cost: $110,000 – Probability: 15%
- Equipment Replacements: Total Cost: $67,000 – Probability: 60%

Solutions:

Total Cost: Computer System	$35,000
Probability of occurrence	30%
Budget for KUs for: Computer System	**$10,500**

Total Cost: Building Repairs	$110,000
Probability of occurrence	15%
Budget for KUs for: Building Repairs	**$16,500**

Total Cost: Equipment Replacements	$67,000
Probability of occurrence	60%
Budget for KUs for: Equipment Replacements	**$40,200**

Total:

Budget for KUs for: Trucks	$200,000
Budget for KUs for: Computer System	$10,500
Budget for KUs for: Building Repairs	$16,500
Budget for KUs for: Equipment Replacements	$40,200
Total Budget for Known-Unknowns	**$267,200**

Debrief:

$267,200 is the total amount COMPANY SUPERTOP must budget for all of the probable costs it may sustain in the upcoming year. It is possible that some of the costs above are not incurred. However, if the probability assignments are effective, then they should average out. Again, the experience and expertise of the management team will be a crucial determinant whether or not the total budget for the KUs is on point.

Note:

For this example, we are assuming that variable costs are not a factor and therefore we can dismiss them from this entire budget.

4.5.3. THE UNKNOWN-UNKNOWNS (UUS):

The UUs are those unexpected costs that will befall on an organization in a given year. These extraordinary costs usually include nature's fury such as earthquakes, hurricanes, floods, tornadoes, etc. They may also consist of unexpected contingencies such as lawsuits, riots, vandalisms, etc.

Note:

Most companies will not budget UUs because it is difficult to factor something that no one can predict in the present. However if it happens, will the organization have the funds necessary to bear their cost?

Insight:

There isn't an actual and universal formula available to calculate the UUs. The few leaders who prioritize this budget line item differ extensively when it comes to process and formulas.

From a strategic stance, we will propose the establishment of the UUs at 10% of the previous year's sales volume. For example, if the last year's sales volume for COMPANY SUPERTOP was $2,000,000, then the budget line item for the UUs would be: $200,000. This $200,000 would cover any extraordinary cost not budgeted for the KKs or KUs. If by chance nothing unusual happens, then the company can welcome it as additional profit.

LET'S PUT IT ALL TOGETHER:

Total Budget for Known-Knowns	$1,709,000
Total Budget for Known-Unknowns	$267,200
Total Budget for Unknown-Unknowns	$200,000
Total Operating Budget	**$2,176,200**

Debrief:

$2,716,200 is the Total Operating Budget for COMPANY SUPERTOP for the year 2011. COMPANY SUPERTOP is expected to meet all of its upcoming financial obligations if this amount is generated in Sales.

4.5.4. FINAL STEP: ASSIGN THE MAP:

Now that we have an operating budget for COMPANY SUPERTOP, it is time to make it "Optimum".

Note:

Anytime, you come across the term "Optimum", think of Profitability.

$2,716,200 is the minimum amount required for COMPANY SUPERTOP to Break-Even in 2011. To make this budget optimum, we just have to add a Minimum Acceptable Profit (MAP) as a percentage of the Operating Budget. Let's assume for example that COMPANY SUPERTOP's goal is to earn at least a profit margin of 20%.

Here is the Solution:

Total Operating Budget (TOB)	$2,176,200
Minimum Acceptable Profit = 20% of TOB	$435,240
Optimum Operating Budget	**$2,611,440**

Debrief:

$2,611,440 is the total amount COMPANY SUPERTOP must produce in Sales for the year 2011 in order to cover its immediate cost, prepare for future contingencies, and earn a MAP of 20%.

4.6. INSTALL A CYCLICAL INVENTORY SYSTEM:
Cost Benefit Analysis should be the driving force when speculating.

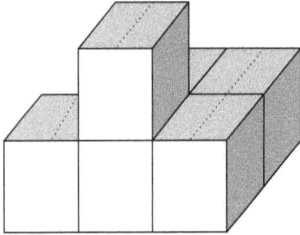

There are many different methods available to manage inventory. The most effective will always involve attention to detail, offer a precise accounting of the volume at any given point in time, and provide useful information to decision makers regarding reorder points. In other words, they will utilize not only present-day information, but look back at historical trends and projected future business volumes and prices in order to help in making purchase choices when the information is useful and relevant.

Cyclical Inventory Systems have proven to be the most efficient. This is especially true for the organizations offering indirect products. A cyclical inventory system is achievable if a solid management system is in place that emphasizes the usage of systematic formulas that would calculate the right amount of inventory to have on shelf on any given day. There are multitudes of software applications available to help calculate current and future inventory needs. However, the available technology alone is not sufficient for the implementation of successful cyclical inventory systems.

Insight:

The cyclical inventory system is difficult to maintain without a certain level of continuity and commitment. Many managers who choose to implement a cyclical system begin with the best of intentions. But then something unexpected happens, and a "temporary" deviation is deemed acceptable in "extenuating" circumstances. There are two problems with this exception, however. First, it detracts from the overall reliability of the cyclical system's records, as these rely on a continuous flow of accurate information. Secondly, once the system's integrity is breached, it becomes that much more difficult to return it to a prime operating condition.

For instance, let's assume that a major supplier offered a one-time discount on all of its products. The less disciplined managers would jump with excitement and buy as much as they can. In their minds, these types of deals do not come often. So why not stock up when the opportunity arises? The logic in this scenario is that it makes perfect business sense to stockpile cheap inventories. There is the problem! The Top Manager, however, is able to maintain composure. He recognizes instantly that the savings available through stocking up on the cheap products can easily be undone by elevated costs associated with handling, holding, and overall management of higher levels of inventory. Before you make the decision to buy a lot when the market is low, be sure to conduct a cost-benefit analysis as to all of the "unanticipated" or indirect costs that will result from your decision.

Example:

We will use the following scenario to elaborate further on the importance of a cyclical inventory system tied to a cost-benefit analysis.

Let's assume the following about COMPANY SUPERTOP's inventory structure and the current "savings" associated with purchasing new inventory—it is by the way, **$4,500:**

Total current used space in square feet	10,000
New inventory space requirement in square feet**	3000
*Savings achieved from buying new inventory	**$4,500**
Handling cost of new inventory	$2,700
Current Monthly Rent	$10,000

Debrief:

Let's take a moment to examine this example in some more detail. Here are the main elements of the problem so far …

A. COMPANY SUPERTOP is paying $10,000 per month to rent 10,000 square feet, which amounts to $1/sq.
B. The new inventory space requirement is 3000 square feet or $3,000.
C. With inventory, also come handling costs, which are usually the labor and packaging costs required to shelve properly the new inventory. In this example, it is $2700.

Let's Solve it. Here we are holding everything else constant:

Current Cost of Space per Square Feet	
Monthly Rent	$10,000
Total Available Space in Square Feet	10,000
Current Monthly Price Per Square Feet	$1.00

New Inventory Cost	
Space Requirement = 3000 * $1	$3,000
Handling cost of new inventory	$2,700
True Cost of New Inventory	**$5,700**

New inventory Cost Benefit Analysis	
New Inventory Savings from Discount	$4,500
True cost of New inventory	$5,700
Actual Benefit/Loss	**($1,200)**

Debrief:

COMPANY SUPERTOP will actually lose $1,200 if it purchases the new inventory. Even if COMPANY SUPERTOP broke-even because of the new purchase, it is still a bad decision. The savings must be large enough to justify the cost and effort associated with increase in new inventory. **This simple example demonstrates the importance of always associating the purchase of new inventory with a cost-benefit analysis.**

4.7. INSTALL AN EFFICIENT RECEIVABLES COLLECTION SYSTEM:
Nobody should keep your money in their pockets.

Every company survives because of the income it receives from selling its products or services. Sounds obvious, right? Perhaps not. Many companies are in such a hurry to "make the sale", that the correct amount of preparation and forethought is not undertaken when selling goods and services on credit. Of course, selling on credit is imperative to generating business volume. Many smaller companies are going to need to finance large asset purchases like heavy machinery, buildings, or other capital assets. Many larger companies conduct so much business that it is impractical to do so through the course of several thousand small transactions. In either case, it seems to make more sense to extend credit to these types of entities, and collect in 15, 30, or 60 days. Accordingly, the development of an effective accounts receivable system is clearly a major operational priority.

Insight:

In many organizations, late payments or non-payments of receivables are devastating from an operational standpoint because they tend to squeeze the cash account and therefore, managerial functions. Furthermore, they undermine short and long-term tactical planning.

Question:

Is it realistic to collect 100% of all accounts receivables?

Answer:

Yes. Despite conventional wisdom, it is ABSOLUTELY a reasonable expectation to "recoup" 100% of your receivables. The system you will put in place will determine the recovery success. Secondly, your attitude as a Top Manager is to produce always above average results. Why then, would you AIM to achieve less than the best possible? You are essentially setting yourself up for mediocrity. You can never settle for second-rate results. You should always reside in the land of excellence and have the "Yes it is possible" approach.

Process:

Of course, there are many considerations you need to acknowledge when developing a 100% collection model. This is not to say that this will necessarily be the most feasible, as achieving the optimal rate will involve a trade-off between business volume and collectability. However, this discussion is to address the process for collecting receivables in its purest form. The following two processes will create a solid framework for an efficient accounts receivable program.

4.7.1. A. CUSTOMER ACCEPTANCE METHODOLOGY:
Not everyone can buy what you sell.

The "Customer Acceptance Methodology" represents the main issue in most collection systems. Many organizations could increase substantially their recovery percentage if they could only sell to those customers who can "fully" buy their products/services. "Fully" means having the willingness to buy WITH the purchasing power to pay in full when the invoice comes due. This is fundamentally a front-end rather than a back-end issue. If for example, an organization sells high-priced luxury items yet the majority of its customer base earns average incomes, then it is very likely that the receivables' recovery percentage will be low.

Many sales managers do not fully understand the true meaning of "*Targeted Marketing*". Most of them believe that targeted marketing only refers to finding those customers who would be interested in buying a company's products/services. These Sales Managers are only excited about the "Sale". These managers haven't recognized that targeted marketing also means attracting those customers who possess the requisite purchasing power.

Therefore, any accounts receivable programs must have a strong control mechanism to prevent the company from selling to customers who cannot "fully" purchase its products/services. And yes, the installation of this control can be painful because many potential customers may be turned away. This is one of the times when your mental toughness should prevail. Why? Because you understand the necessity to remain strong and disciplined regardless of the difficult choices you face.

4.7.2. TRIGGER MECHANISMS:
Everyone should be treated the same.

Trigger Mechanisms refer to those sets of actions that will take effect over the life of an invoice. An invoice can have a positive or delinquent lifespan. The main goals for these trigger mechanisms are to promote consistently a positive life of an invoice. A trigger can either be an e-mail reminder, a phone call, a personal visit, a payment plan enrollment, etc. Each trigger should go in effect based the actual situation of each invoice. For the purpose of this book, it is unfeasible to go in details with each possible trigger.

However, we will outline some essential guidelines to follow when implementing these triggers:

UNIFORMITY:

Each customer is to be treated as a potential delinquent case. Even if the customer has had a positive history with the organization, the trigger should still assume the worst-case scenario. This rule will prevent those responsible for collecting accounts receivable from establishing their personal procedures. The goal here is to eliminate ambiguity.

AUTOMATION:

Automating triggers will prevent human errors and guarantees on-time delivery, which will contribute to the positive life of an invoice.

4.8. DEVELOP EFFICIENT QUALITY CONTROL STANDARDS:
Effective branding is about providing exactly what you advertise.

Quality Control Standards (QCS) ensure excellence in the delivery of products/services. With strong QCS, a company will remain competitive and grow its consumer base, and therefore develop a strong brand. The reason why many companies do not favor a complete implementation of robust QCS is because they could become costly and may require additional personnel. This goes back to the concept of cost-benefit analysis. For many companies, the cost is too great and usually the benefits are not easily quantifiable. Accordingly, the majority of companies settle with slim and inefficient QCS.

Here is the Best Process to use:

4.8.1. A. EFFICIENT SAMPLING:
There is a million ways to waste your time.

In order to determine if the delivery of products/services is in accord to acceptable standards, an efficient sampling method is required. Larger companies that produce millions of widgets for example, cannot inspect every item individually. It is simply impossible for obvious reasons. As a result, a sampling method must be implemented which primary function is to represent the entire production/servicing output. There is a multitude of sampling methods used by companies and you should educate yourself on some of them. However, the sampling mechanisms that are the most effective are those that simply reduce strategically sampling errors.

Example:

Let's assume that COMPANY SUPERTOP manufactures CD players. As a sampling method, COMPANY SUPERTOP decides that every tenth CD player will be inspected by a quality inspector located in a specific location along the assembly process. Let's also assume that this sampling method is active at all times throughout the assembly process. Lastly, we will also assume that this inspection of the sample is the only quality control system in place. With this sampling method, COMPANY SUPERTOP hopes to catch every deficiency in the production line. Can you envision some potential sampling errors?

Here is the answer:

This sampling method has a big problem. On the surface, it seems to possess an acceptable sampling method. However, it lacks randomness, which makes it ineffective. Let's assume for example that the main production equipment is wrongly programmed and produces a faulty CD player every eighth copy. This means that COMPANY SUPERTOP may never catch this error and possibly every customer who buys every eighth CD player produced will be calling the merchandise return department.

This sampling error could have been avoided using the following system for example:

- On Monday, every tenth copy will be inspected—On Tuesday, every ninth copy—On Wednesday, every eighth, and so on.
- Alternatively, COMPANY SUPERTOP could have changed the sequence based on the time of the day.
- Or even, change randomly the formula every hour

The best strategy is to develop constant randomness, which will bear higher success of detecting potential production errors.

4.8.2. CORRECTION STRATEGY:
Ready Before is better than Ready After.

The Correction Strategy is the plan of action ready for activation in the event of the discovery of undesired standards. It is critical that this plan of action is well crafted and outlined in advance so not to halt the production/servicing schedule. Therefore, when a snag is found, a plan is already in place to fix it.

Note:

An emergency brainstorming/strategy session is impractical during a moment of crisis because it leads to the implementation of unproved systems.

4.8.3. INCENTIVES:

It's good to throw a bone once a while.

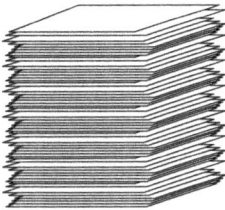

An efficient QCS should always include an incentive system to encourage the participation of everyone in the organization. In many organizations, the top-level managers will rely only on the QCS they have implemented to catch every error in the production/servicing. It is without doubt a very bad approach. In addition to the company's standards, the good managers will also seek to spur the critical thinking ability of each employee. These managers understand that their employees are an essential source in the improvement of quality. Consequently, they need to be incentivized to trigger their willingness to participate actively in the process. Monetary or promotion incentives are of course on top of the list. For example, a company may have as a policy to promote immediately an employee who finds significant errors in the production of products. Alternatively, the policy may be to reward employees with bonus payments if they develop strategies that would reduce production errors.

4.9. DEVELOP OPTIMUM DISTRIBUTION CHANNELS (ODCS):

Selling is a Route with multiple shortcuts.

Optimum Distributions Channels (ODCs) represent the best supply avenues a company can establish. ODCs are extremely critical in the operational process of an organization because the decisions to set up specific avenues will determine the aptitude to generate consistent profits. This concept is very simple but its efficient implementation is less certain in most organizations. Some managers believe that their best strategy is to open as many supply chains as possible and try to sell their products/services to everyone. However, they tend not to analyze if each distribution channel can produce the expected minimum level of profitability.

We can spend an entire chapter on this subject outlining the various models used by different companies. However, a short and precise strategic model will suffice for our purpose.

Note:

The best strategy available is Return on Investment (ROI) Approach.

Example:

COMPANY SUPERTOP produces four types of electronics (CD Players, DVD Players, Radios, and TVs). Furthermore, COMPANY SUPERTOP uses only four distribution channels to sells its products. The production, revenues, and channels are shown in the chart below.

Products	Production Cost	Revenue	Channel
CD Players	$350,000	$425,000	1
DVD Players	$475,000	$625,000	2
Radios	$180,000	$205,000	3
TVs	$720,000	$965,000	4

4.9.1. RETURN ON INVESTMENT (ROI):

This will never get old.

To calculate the ROI, divide each revenue stream by its cost of production. See chart below.

Products	Production Cost	Revenue	Channel	**ROI**
CD Players	$350,000	$425,000	1	**$1.21**
DVD Players	$475,000	$625,000	2	**$1.32**
Radios	$180,000	$205,000	3	**$1.14**
TVs	$720,000	$965,000	4	**$1.34**

Debrief:

$1.21 means that for every $1 spent in the production of CD players, COMPANY SUPERTOP received $1.21 in return. As you can tell, TVs bear the highest ROI, which is $1.34.

Note:

Obviously, from this straightforward illustration, it seems that COMPANY SUPERTOP should invest its entire budget in the production of TVs and sell only in Channel 4. However, this strategy may not be as easy to implement because of the following reasons:

- The demand may not exist to accommodate more supply for this product line in this channel
- The channel may be contractually saturated. This means that vendors are contractually obligated to receive supplies from other companies
- Every other company will see the benefit and start producing TVs only and selling in this channel, which will drive prices down and erase further profit-making ability

Digging Deeper:

First, let's calculate the direct profit margins for each product line.

Let's assume the following:

Product	Prod. Cost	Revenue	Profit	Profit %	Channel	ROI
CDs	$350,000	$425,000	$75,000	15.15%	1	$1.21
DVDs	$475,000	$625,000	$150,000	30.30%	2	$1.32
Radios	$180,000	$205,000	$25,000	5.05%	3	$1.14
TVs	$720,000	$965,000	$245,000	49.49%	4	$1.34

Let's also assume that each channel is saturated and COMPANY SUPERTOP cannot increase its supply in other channels.

With this assumption, it shouldn't make sense to change the product lines and distribution channels regardless of the profit margin. Even the product with the lowest ROI (Radios: $1.14) is still profitable ($25,000). This is the belief system of many supply chain managers. As long as a product line is profitable, it makes sense to keep it alive.

However, if you analyze critically the table above, you can perhaps determine that Radios in Channel 3 could be eliminated.

The Reasoning:

Even though Radios are profitable, the following cost/benefit analysis must be performed:

- Does a 5.05% in the profit group justify the investment? Simply put, is it worth the trouble?
- Could the $180,000 for the production of radios be used for something else such as research for example, which has proven to increase a company's competitive ability?
- Will the operational process improve if **One** product line is eliminated?
- Will the staff become more productive because they will have to specialize only in 3 products instead of 4

Best Strategy:

Holding everything else constant, the best strategy is to eliminate the production of radios and supply channel 3. A straightforward cost/benefit analysis would agree.

4.10. DEVELOP THE BEST SALES STRATEGY:

A Strategy is part art, part system.

Example:

Consider a car dealership that sells used and new vehicles. Furthermore, this dealership has the space to accommodate only 100 cars at once. This is a single channel because the cars are sold only from one location. Therefore, it becomes more of an issue of sales margins rather than distribution channels strategy.

Note:

With single channels, the issues revolve product configurations and market positioning.

The management of the dealership must determine the following:

1. The number of cars to have in the lot at a time (inventory)
2. The percentage of new and used cars to have in the lot (lot configuration)
3. The brand, type, and average price of each car (target marketing)
4. Accordingly, a complete consumer, industry, and market analysis is necessary to find these answers.

Note:

There isn't a shortcut formula that would answer these questions effectively. The entire research—sometimes costly must be completed. This is the reason why many smaller companies will bypass this research because of limited resources. Unfortunately, they end up making the decisions above without verifiable intelligence.

Let's illustrate the importance of the following research:

Let's assume the consumer, industry, and market researches were completed and the following were the findings:

The Consumer Profile:

1. Age: 37 years
2. Median Income: $47,000/year
3. Gender: Male
4. Marital Status: Single
5. Type of preferred car: Used 4-door Sedan
6. Education Level: High School
7. Interests: Sports and leisure

The Industry Profile:

1. Trend: Cars from Europe are very popular
2. Barriers to entry: None
3. Selling Channels: In physical lots and online
4. Car assembly locations: East Coast of the US and China
5. Opportunities: High mileage efficiency and electric cars

Market Profile (Companies in direct competition):

1. Average lot capacity: 95 cars
2. Average selling price: $7500
3. Average number of employees in a dealership: 17
4. Management Experience: More than 15 years
5. Types of car sold: Used Sedan
6. Average number of car sold per month: 55

Note:

As seen in the three analyses above, an ample amount of information is available to establish the Sales strategy for the car dealership. **Here they are:**

Consumer:

The median income for the typical consumer is $47,000. This means that selling less expensive cars is the best strategy. The typical consumer couldn't afford for example, a $100,000 new Mercedes Benz.

Lot configuration:

Since the consumer and market analyses establish that the typical consumer wants a cheap used car, it would make sense to have more used cars rather than new ones in the lot. For example, the lot configuration strategy could be: 70% of the cars to be of used condition and 30% of new condition. Without this information, the car dealership could have had perhaps 30% of cars to be of used condition and would believe it was a good strategy.

Market:

From a competitive standpoint, the car dealership cannot sell vehicles over $7,500 because its consumer base will go buy from its competitors. Therefore, an average car price shouldn't exceed $7,500.

Industry:

The industry analysis stipulates that high mileage efficiency and electric vehicles will be the market to attack in the near and distant future. As a result, the car dealership should start establishing a process by which it will acquire these cars either from the east coast of the US or in China.

Overall Strategy:

The consumer, industry, and market analyses dictate that the best strategy in the future will be: *to sell used high-mileage/electric cars with an average price of $7,500*. The only possible route to reach this specific conclusion is through the analyses performed above.

4.11. DETERMINE THE OPTIMUM NUMBER OF LOCATIONS:

A good "Where" Strategy is your compass of success.

The number and placement of locations is a key determinant of a company's market share and profits levels. What makes it "optimum" is the presence of some verifiable assurance that the existence of each location is financially advantageous. In basic terms, a clear and honest assessment of the "optimum number of locations" will dictate which locations need to be shut down and where you need to open the next one. Goals assessment, resource assessment, market analysis, and forecasting are the four major tools utilized to determine the optimum number of locations.

Goals assessment:

The concept of "Goals Assessment" refers to the financial ambitions of a company. For example, a company may only wish to increase its profit levels in the next five years.

The optimum number of locations would differ if the company's primary objective was to increase its market share, and profit levels were a secondary concern. The strategies for increasing market penetration and elevating profits may often overlap, but can easily diverge when the objectives clash with one another. In either case, the strategies may differ.

For instance, a company that was solely focused on increasing profit margin may choose to invest in making its existing locations more efficient. It may choose to increase revenues at existing locations only. The approach would include the implementation of strategies that would eliminate efficiency problems by using targeted systems and controls. Furthermore, this strategy may also establish the necessity to close certain number of locations that couldn't conform to the minimum efficiency standard.

On the other hand, if the goal were to increase market share only, it would make sense for the company to open as many locations as possible with the hope of gaining new customers. The company may even choose to establish these new locations as "loss leaders" and enter the market by selling at razor thin profit margins to encourage sales and therefore, get noticed by its prospective clientele. This is a popular strategy for those companies who are interested in driving out their competition. These companies would open locations next or near their competitions and slash their prices. It frequently results in price wars and the company with the higher financial strength (Wealth) would survive.

Resource Assessment:

Opening new locations costs money. Operating existing locations costs money. Closing existing locations costs money. And each of these choices has an impact on balance sheet AND income statement line items. In other words, the choice will affect existing resources, and the potential for accumulating future resources. This calls for an adept assessment as to how resources are to be allocated. The financial burden of opening new locations can be so great that it could put an unprepared company out of business. It is crucial to play out a variety of scenarios to determine how sensitive the overall operation is to the addition of new locations or retraction of those already in existence.

The company must determine how far it can stretch its cash reserves. Are resources plentiful enough to sustain an operation that breaks-even or even possibly loses money at first? Even worse, can your business model survive the possibility of an outright failure of the new location? Even with limited resources, some companies still choose to expand through the usage of credit either from their bank or from investors. It is imperative to have a rock-solid, unassailable, almost foolproof strategy when undertaking this precarious route. Many companies have gone bankrupt by way of ambition. They threw the dice and lost it all when "calculated risks" actually resulted in financial bondage that was too enormous to overcome. The basic rule of thumb when expanding is to utilize the resources a company *can afford to lose* without disturbing its chances of survival.

Market Analysis:

A thorough market analysis will be helpful if the primary goal is to add more locations and as a result, increase market share. In this case, the expected demand, and the channel saturation will be the main components of this analysis.

On the demand side, the analysis should determine if the products/services the company sells would interest a consumer's group. In simple terms, a company may have the resources to open new locations but may not be able to generate the demand necessary to justify the investment. Conducting random consumer surveys may be the best analysis tools.

Channel saturation refers to the supply side. It may be difficult for a company to increase its market share in a specific location if other suppliers overcrowd it. The result may just result in unending price wars.

APPENDIX:

APPENDIX 1: COMPARATIVE COST ANALYSIS:

We will develop a detailed a Profit & Loss (P&L) to derive a complete Comparative Cost Analysis. It is at least a minimum requirement that you cultivate a comfort level when reading and analyzing a P&L statement.

Assume the following about COMPANY SUPERTOP:

- Limited Liability Company
- 30% taxable rate
- P&L for 4 years starting in 2005
- The executives in charge own the company

Gross Profit:

Table 1.1

Description	2005	2006	2007	2008
Gross Sales	$2,000,000	$1,500,000	$2,700,000	$3,000,000
Discounts/Rebates	-$50,000	-$60,000	-$70,000	-$80,000
Net Sales	**$1,950,000**	**$1,440,000**	**$2,630,000**	**$2,920,000**
Direct Material Cost	$320,000	$265,000	$431,000	$345,000
Direct Labor Cost	$150,000	$120,000	$295,000	$302,000
Other Direct Costs	$8,000	$12,000	$11,000	$14,000
Total Cost Of Sales	$478,000	$397,000	$737,000	$661,000
Gross Profit	**$1,472,000**	**$1,043,000**	**$1,893,000**	**$2,259,000**

Review:

The discounts and rebates are subtracted from the gross sales to obtain the Net Sales. For accounting and reporting purposes, many companies choose to include them into their P&L to elevate their revenues. It serves to impress potential investors.

The Formulas:

NET SALES = GROSS SALES — DISCOUNTS/REBATES
TOTAL COST OF SALES = DIRECT MATERIAL COST +
DIRECT LABOR COST + OTHER DIRECT COSTS
GROSS PROFIT = NET SALES — TOTAL COST OF SALES

Expenses (Investments):

Fixed Expenses:

Table 2.1

Description	2005	2006	2007	2008
Executive Salaries	$155,000	$165,000	$195,000	$205,000
Advertising	$50,000	$51,500	$53,050	$54,640
Auto & Truck Expense	$30,000	$30,900	$31,800	$32,800
Depreciation	$5,000	$5,150	$45,300	$50,500
Employee Benefits	$3,000	$3,090	$3,180	$3,280
Outside Business Expense	$1,000	$1,030	$1,060	$1,090
Insurance	$3,910	$3,750	$4,010	$3,990
Bank Charges	$2,130	$2,200	$2,260	$2,330
Legal & Professional Serv.	$1,000	$1,330	$1,670	$2,020
Meals & Entertainment	$4,000	$4,120	$4,240	$4,370
Office Expense	$6,000	$6,180	$6,370	$6,560
Retirement Plans	$1,000	$1,030	$1,060	$1,090
Rent – Equipment	$3,000	$3,090	$3,180	$3,280
Rent – Office	$8,750	$9,110	$9,540	$9,930
Repairs	$1,000	$1,030	$1,060	$1,090
Supplies	$1,000	$1,030	$1,060	$1,090
Payroll	$1,000	$1,030	$1,060	$1,090
Travel	$6,230	$6,120	$6,010	$5,900
Utilities	$12,000	$12,400	$14,200	$17,000
Other Expenses	$25,000	$33,000	$15,000	$22,000
Total Fixed Costs	$320,020	$342,090	$400,110	$429,050

Variable Costs:

Table 2.2

Description	2005	2006	2007	2008
Office Salaries	$90,000	$102,700	$112,400	$118,600
Employee Benefits	$43,000	$46,880	$47,970	$51,250
Payroll Taxes	$18,000	$18,540	$19,100	$19,670
Sales & Marketing	$14,000	$14,420	$14,850	$15,300
Telephone	$6,000	$6,180	$6,370	$6,560
Office Supplies	$2,110	$2,680	$3,010	$3,490
Bad Debts	$100	$100	$110	$110
Postage	$5,560	$5,720	$5,900	$6,070
Total Variable Costs	$178,770	$197,220	$209,710	$221,050

Operating Income:

Operating Income after Interest, Depreciation, and Amortization.

Table 3.1

Description	2005	2006	2007	2008
Operating Exp.	$498,790	$539,310	$609,820	$650,100
Interest	$16,300	$16,700	$17,200	$17,800
Depreciation	$32,500	$33,500	$34,500	$35,500
Amortization	$1,250	$1,290	$1,330	$1,370
Total expenses	$548,840	$590,800	$662,850	$704,770
Operating Income	$923,160	$452,200	$1,230,150	$1,554,230

Review:

OPERATING INCOME = GROSS PROFIT (TABLE 1.1) —
TOTAL EXPENSES (TABLE 3.1)
OPERATING INCOME AFTER GAIN/LOSS ON SALE OF
ASSETS = OPERATING INCOME +/- GAIN/LOSS

Table 3.2

Description	2005	2006	2007	2008
Gain/Loss	$10,000	$10,300	$10,600	$10,900
Other (Net)	$20,000	$20,600	$21,200	$31,900
Income Before Tax	**$953,160**	**$483,100**	**$1,261,950**	**$1,597,030**

Net Income and Return on Ownership:

Table 4.1

Description	2005	2006	2007	2008
Income Before Tax	$953,160	$483,100	$1,261,950	$1,597,030
Income Tax	$285,948	$144,930	$378,585	$479,109
Net Income	$667,212	$338,170	$883,365	$1,117,921
Return On Ownership	**$822,212**	**$503,170**	**$1,078,365**	**$1,322,921**

Debrief:

A. Income Taxes: We assumed earlier a taxable rate of 30%. Therefore in 2005 for example: $953,160 * 30% = $285,948

B. Net Income = Income before tax — tax. In 2005, it is: $953,160 — $285,948 = $667, 212

C. Return on Ownership = Net Income + Executive Salaries (Table 2.1)

For example in 2005, the Return On Ownership = $667,212 + $155,000 = $822,212.

Since we have assumed that the executives own the company, it makes absolute sense to add their salaries to the net income.

Putting it All Together:

Here is the complete P&L for COMPANY SUPERTOP:

Description	2005	2006	2007	2008
Gross Sales	$2,000,000	$1,500,000	$2,700,000	$3,000,000
Discounts	-$50,000	-$60,000	-$70,000	-$80,000
Net Sales	$1,950,000	$1,440,000	$2,630,000	$2,920,000
Direct Material Cost	$320,000	$265,000	$431,000	$345,000
Direct Labor Cost	$150,000	$120,000	$295,000	$302,000
Other Direct Cost	$8,000	$12,000	$11,000	$14,000
(COGS)	$478,000	$397,000	$737,000	$661,000
Gross Profit	**$1,472,000**	**$1,043,000**	**$1,893,000**	**$2,259,000**
Executive Salaries	$155,000	$165,000	$195,000	$205,000
Advertising	$50,000	$51,500	$53,050	$54,640
Auto & Truck Expenses	$30,000	$30,900	$31,800	$32,800
Depreciation	$5,000	$5,150	$45,300	$50,500
Employee Benefits	$3,000	$3,090	$3,180	$3,280
Outside Business Exp.	$1,000	$1,030	$1,060	$1,090
Insurance	$3,910	$3,750	$4,010	$3,990
Bank Fees	$2,130	$2,200	$2,260	$2,330
Legal & Prof. Fees	$1,000	$1,330	$1,670	$2,020
Meals & Entertainment	$4,000	$4,120	$4,240	$4,370
Office Expenses	$6,000	$6,180	$6,370	$6,560
Retirement Plans	$1,000	$1,030	$1,060	$1,090
Rental Equipment	$3,000	$3,090	$3,180	$3,280
Rental Property	$8,750	$9,110	$9,540	$9,930
Repairs	$1,000	$1,030	$1,060	$1,090
Supplies	$1,000	$1,030	$1,060	$1,090
Other Taxes	$1,000	$1,030	$1,060	$1,090
Travel	$6,230	$6,120	$6,010	$5,900
Utilities	$12,000	$12,400	$14,200	$17,000

Other Expenses	$25,000	$33,000	$15,000	$22,000
Total Fixed Costs	**$320,020**	**$342,090**	**$400,110**	**$429,050**
Office Salaries	$90,000	$102,700	$112,400	$118,600
Employee Benefits	$43,000	$46,880	$47,970	$51,250
Payroll Taxes	$18,000	$18,540	$19,100	$19,670
Sales And Mark	$14,000	$14,420	$14,850	$15,300
Telephone	$6,000	$6,180	$6,370	$6,560
Office Supplies	$2,110	$2,680	$3,010	$3,490
Bad Debts	$100	$100	$110	$110
Postage	$5,560	$5,720	$5,900	$6,070
Total Variable Costs	**$178,770**	**$197,220**	**$209,710**	**$221,050**
Total Operating Exp.	**$498,790**	**$539,310**	**$609,820**	**$650,100**
Interest	$16,300	$16,700	$17,200	$17,800
Depreciation	$32,500	$33,500	$34,500	$35,500
Amortization	$1,250	$1,290	$1,330	$1,370
Total Expenses	$548,840	$590,800	$662,850	$704,770
Operating Income	**$923,160**	**$452,200**	**$1,230,150**	**$1,554,230**
Gain/Loss Assets	$10,000	$10,300	$10,600	$10,900
Other (Net)	$20,000	$20,600	$21,200	$31,900
Income Before Tax	$953,160	$483,100	$1,261,950	$1,597,030
Income Taxes	$285,948	$144,930	$378,585	$479,109
Net Income	**$667,212**	**$338,170**	**$883,365**	**$1,117,921**
Return/Owners	**$822,212**	**$503,170**	**$1,078,365**	**$1,322,921**

Bottom Line:

Many companies, large or small, will use various models of Profit & Loss Statements. Some will use a model that their accountants have put in place for reporting purposes. Others will use a template they created because it made sense to them. However, the model shown above is amongst the most universally acceptable. It facilitates the financial analysis process, and is applicable in a variety of different environments, industries, and applications.

Every income and expense item is allocated in a sequential format that makes sense from a readability standpoint.

With the P&L statement above, we are able to develop the Comparative Cost Analysis for every expense, (which as we have discussed are in fact "investments") COMPANY SUPERTOP incurred from 2005 to 2008.

Direct Labor:

		Year	Year	Year	Year
		2005	2006	2007	2008
	Gross Sales	$2,000,000	$1,500,000	$2,700,000	$3,000,000
	Direct Labor	$150,000	$120,000	$295,000	$302,000
R O I	Direct Labor	$13.33	$12.50	$9.15	$9.93

Best Period

Ideal Cost (Sales/Best Period of Return)

	IDEAL COST	CURRENT COST	ANNUAL LOSS
2005	$150,000	$150,000	$0
2006	$112,500	$120,000	$7,500
2007	$202,500	$295,000	$92,500
2008	$225,000	$302,000	$77,000
		Total	**Loss**
		$177,000	

Debrief:

The best year of efficiency or ROI occurred in 2005 and the total loss for the next three years is $177,000.

Sales And Marketing:

		Year	Year	Year	Year
		2005	2006	2007	2008
	Gross Sales	$2,000,000	$1,500,000	$2,700,000	$3,000,000
	S & M	$14,000	$14,420	$14,850	$15,300
R					
O	S &M	**$142.86**	**$104.02**	**$181.82**	**$196.08**
I					

Best Period

Ideal Cost (Sales/Best Period of Return)

	IDEAL COST	CURRENT COST	ANNUAL LOSS
2005	$10,200	$14,000	$3,800
2006	$7,650	$14,420	$6,770
2007	$13,770	$14,850	$1,080
2008	$15,300	$15,300	$0
		Total Loss	$11,650

Debrief:

COMPANY SUPERTOP spent $11,650 more than needed in Sales and Marketing from 2005 to 2008.

Practice:

Now that you have mastered this process, calculate all of the cost over-runs for COMPANY SUPERTOP.

Use the table below to check your answers. Some costs in the P&L shown above were excluded because their impact was insignificant.

Direct Material Cost	$303,000		Travel	$6,167
Direct Labor Cost	$177,000		Utilities	$7,215
Other Direct Costs	$8,200		Other Expenses	$43,889
Advertising	$41,627		Office salaries	$59,993
Auto & Truck Expenses	$24,913		Employee benefits	$31,933
Depreciation	$82,950		Payroll taxes	$14,989
Employee Benefits	$2,491		Sales and Marketing	$11,650
Outside Business Expenses	$837		Telephone	$4,993
Insurance	$3,424		Office supplies	$1,584
Bank Charges	$1,775		Bad debts	$83
Professional Fees	$3,329		Postage	$4,635
Office Expense	$4,993		Interest	$13,413
Retirement Plans	$837		Depreciation	$27,133
Rental Equipment	$2,491		Amortization	$1,039
Rental Property	$6,878		**Total Loss**	**$894,299**
Repairs	$837			

Total Loss:

As the total shows, COMPANY SUPERTOP overspent $894,299 from 2005 to 2008. This analysis is very critical because it demonstrates what profit level a company could have enjoyed if the highest returns were the standards.

APPENDIX 2: Z-SCORE ANALYSIS:

We will need the information from the **P&L** (we will use the one above outlined in the CCA) and **Balance Sheet** (See Below) to develop the Z-Score Analysis.

Assets:

Assets	Year	Year	Year	Year
Current Assets	*2005*	*2006*	*2007*	*2008*
Cash In Bank Account	$451,000	$465,000	$478,000	$493,000
Accounts Receivable	$350,000	$461,000	$871,000	$1,380,000
Notes Receivable	$1,200	$3,200	$3,000	$3,400
Inventory	$400,000	$612,000	$824,000	$937,000
Other Current Assets	$10,000	$10,300	$10,600	$10,900
Total Current Assets	**$1,212,200**	**$1,551,500**	**$2,186,600**	**$2,824,300**
Fixed Assets	*2005*	*2006*	*2007*	*2008*
Land	$1,000,000	$1,030,000	$1,110,000	$1,110,000
Buildings	$1,500,000	$1,050,000	$1,590,000	$1,740,000
Equipment	$800,000	$824,000	$949,000	$874,000
Subtotal	**$3,300,000**	**$2,904,000**	**$3,649,000**	**$3,724,000**
Less-Accumulated Dep.	($400,000)	($412,000)	($424,000)	($437,000)
Total Fixed Assets	**$2,900,000**	**$2,492,000**	**$3,225,000**	**$3,287,000**
Intangible Assets	*2005*	*2006*	*2007*	*2008*
Investment	$50,000	$51,500	$53,000	$54,600
Less-Accumulated Amount	$20,000	$20,600	$21,200	$21,900
Total Intangible Assets	**$30,000**	**$30,900**	**$31,800**	**$32,700**
Other Assets	$25,000	$25,800	$26,500	$27,300
Total Assets	**$4,167,200**	**$4,100,200**	**$5,469,900**	**$6,171,300**

Liabilities and Equity:

Liabilities And Equity	Year	Year	Year	Year
Current Liabilities	2005	2006	2007	2008
Accounts Payable	$600,000	$618,000	$637,000	$641,000
Notes Payable	$100,000	$103,000	$106,000	$109,000
Portion Of Long-Term Debt	$100,000	$103,000	$106,000	$109,000
Income Taxes	$30,000	$30,900	$31,800	$32,800
Accrued Expenses	$90,000	$92,700	$95,500	$98,300
Other Current Liabilities	$16,000	$16,500	$17,000	$17,500
Total Current Liabilities	**$936,000**	**$964,100**	**$993,300**	**$1,007,600**
Non-Current Liabilities	*2005*	*2006*	*2007*	*2008*
Long-Term Debt	$601,000	$624,000	$646,000	$668,000
Deferred Income	$100,000	$103,000	$106,000	$109,000
Deferred Income Taxes	$30,000	$30,900	$31,800	$32,800
Other Long-Term Liabilities	$50,000	$51,500	$53,000	$54,600
Total Liabilities	**$1,717,000**	**$1,773,500**	**$1,830,100**	**$1,872,000**
Stockholders' Equity	*2005*	*2006*	*2007*	*2008*
Stock Issued	$100,000	$100,000	$100,000	$100,000
Additional Paid In Capital	$950,000	$679,000	$1,850,000	$2,470,000
Retained Earnings	*$1,400,200*	*$1,547,700*	*$1,689,800*	*$1,729,300*
Total Stockholders' Equity	**$2,450,200**	**$2,326,700**	**$3,639,800**	**$4,299,300**
Total Liabilities And Equity	**$4,167,200**	**$4,100,200**	**$5,469,900**	**$6,171,300**

Formulas To Memorize:

EQUITY (NET WORTH) = ASSETS — LIABILITIES

RETAINED EARNINGS = ASSETS — LIABILITIES — CAPITAL STOCK + ADDITIONAL PAID IN CAPITAL (APIC)

ENDING RETAINED EARNINGS = BEGINNING RETAINED EARNINGS + NET INCOME + DIVIDENDS PAID

In This Example (2008):

RETAINED EARNINGS = TOTAL ASSETS — TOTAL LIABILITIES — CAPITAL STOCK — ADDITIONAL PAID IN CAPITAL (APIC)

Thus,

RETAINED EARNINGS IN 2008 = $6,171,300 — $1,872,000 —$100,000 — $2,470,000 = $1,729,300

Side Note:

Retained Earnings are the equalizer between Assets and Liabilities + Equity.

THE Z-SCORE FORMULA:

Z –SCORE = 1.2 * **S** + 1.4 * **C** + 3.3 * **O** + 0.6 * **R** + .999 * **E**
S = Working Capital ÷ Total Assets
Working Capital = Current Assets — Current Liabilities
C = Retained Earnings ÷ Total Assets
O = Operating Income ÷ Total Assets
R = Equity ÷ Total Liabilities
E = Sales ÷ Total Assets

Now, let's find the Z-Score for COMPANY SUPERTOP for the year 2008 using the values from the given the financial statements.

Data as given (2008):

- Working Capital = $2,284,300 — $1,007,600 = $1,816,700 and Total Assets = $6,171,300
- Retained Earnings = $1,729,300
- Operating Income = $1,554,230
- Sales = $2,920,000
- Total Assets = $6,171,300
- Net Worth or Equity = $4,299,300
- Total Liability = $1,872,000

Let's Solve It:

SOLUTION:

1.2 * (($2,824,300 — $1,007,600) ÷ $6,171,300))

+

1.4 * ($1,729,300 ÷ $6,171,300)

+

3.3 * ($1,554,230 ÷ $6,171,300)

+

0.6 * ($4,299,300 ÷ $1,872,000)

+

.999 * ($2, 920, 00 ÷ $6,171,300)

Answer:

Z-Score in 2008 = ~3.43

Interpreting the Z-Score:

- If the Z-Score is above 2.99 —— Company is safe from failure
- If the Z-Score is between 1.81 to 2.99 —— Company may have financial troubles
- If the Z-Score is less than 1.81—— Company faces imminent bankruptcy

Good News:

The Z-Score is 3.43 and higher than 2.99.

We can therefore assume that COMPANY SUPERTOP will be presumably solvent and able to meet all of its financial obligations in the future.

Practice:

Use the following data to solve the Z-Score for COMPANY SUPERTOP.

Current Asset	$3,000,000
Current Liabilities	$5,000,000
Total Assets	$4,000,000
Net Sales	$3,000,000
Total Equity	$2,000,000
Total Liabilities	$7,000,000
Sales	$1,000,000
Retained Earning	$1,500,000
Operating Income	$1,200,000

Answer:

If you solve it correctly, you will find a Z-Score of ~1.34. Since the Z-Score is less than 1.81, we can conclude that COMPANY SUPERTOP is presumably insolvent.

More Practice:

Use the data given in the financial statement to find the Z-Scores for COMPANY SUPERTOP for the years of 2007, 2006, and 2005.

Insight:

You shouldn't consider it acceptable if you complete this analysis and find a very high Z-Score for an organization. It will be a strong sign that things need to be reviewed. Sometimes a Z-Score can be severely skewed by oddities that may hold little relevancy to future operations. For instance, if the balance sheet contains an inflated value on land and equipment or an unusual capital infusion that year, then the Z-score will be distorted. Correspondingly, a lower score doesn't necessarily represent the looming possibility of bankruptcy. The Z-Score is just one of many tools in your arsenal available to measure the general solvency of a company. As a safe strategy, you must always consider all factors before determining whether your Z-Score is truly an accurate representation of the financial viability of your organization.

APPENDIX 3: OPTIMUM BREAK EVEN POINTS:

Example:

From the previous P&L statement, we know the following:

Line	Description	2005
1	Net Sales	$1,950,000
2	Cost of Goods Sold	$478,000
3	Total Variable Costs	$178,770
4	Total Fixed Costs	$370,070
5	Net Profit	$923,160

*L1 means Line 1 as seen above.

Use the following process to calculate Break-Even Points.

Fixed & Variable Costs Portions:

In real life situations, Variable Costs will often overlap with Fixed Costs. It takes an astute manager to know when to classify a cost as one or the other, and this can depend on the situation as well as the period of time over which the cost is analyzed. For example, a company may purchase goods and services to meet its current production requirement and use the remaining portion in other unrelated areas. Therefore, attributing a portion of the Variable Costs to the Fixed Costs makes sense because it takes into account the possible allocation.

In this Break-Even example, we have assumed that half of the Variable Costs were indeed Fixed Costs. Once half of the Variable Costs are added to the Fixed Costs, we will get the Total Fixed Costs, for which we will next calculate the Break-Even point.

Total Fixed Costs:

= FIXED COSTS + (VARIABLE COSTS ÷ 2)
= ($370,070) + ($178,770 ÷ 2) = $459,455

Break-Even Percentage:

= TOTAL FIXED COSTS ÷ (TOTAL FIXED COSTS + NET PROFIT)
= ($459,455) ÷ ($459,455 + $923,160) = 33%

Days to Break-Even:

= BREAK-EVEN PERCENTAGE * 365
= 33% * 365 = ~121 DAYS

Here we assume, 365 days in a year. The result of the above calculation indicates that COMPANY SUPERTOP needs only to operate 121 days in 2005 in order to Break-Even for the entire year. Any income received after the first 121 days of operation is technically a profit.

Days Per Month To Break-Even:

= DAYS IN PERIOD TO BREAK-EVEN ÷ 12
= 121DAYS ÷ 12 = ~10 DAYS

We then divide the number of days by 12 because there are 12 months in a year. Therefore, it took COMPANY SUPERTOP 10 days to Break-Even each month in 2005. This means all costs associated with production have been covered. Anything after day 10 is technically a profit.

Break-Even Amounts:

Below, we calculate Break-Even points for different periods throughout the year.

Yearly Break-Even:

= NET SALES * BREAK-EVEN PERCENTAGE
= $1,950,000 * 33% = $643,500

Monthly Break-Even:

= YEARLY BREAK-EVEN ÷ 12
= $643500 ÷ 12 = $53,625

Weekly Break-Even:

= MONTHLY BREAK-EVEN ÷ (52÷12)
= $53,625 ÷ (52÷12) = $12,375

*52 represents the number of weeks in a year and 12, the number of months. On average, there are approximately 4.3 weeks in a month.

Daily Break-Even:

= WEEKLY BREAK-EVEN ÷ 5
= $12,375 ÷ 5 = $2,475

*Assuming a 5-day workweek.

Hourly Break-Even:

= DAILY BREAK-EVEN ÷ 8
= $2,492 ÷ 8 = $309

*Assuming an 8-hour workday.

Break-Even Date:

Net Sales	$1,950,000
Total Fixed Costs	$459,455
Net Profit	$923,160
Break-Even %	33%
Break-Even Amount	$643,500
*Break-Even Date	**April 30**

= BREAK-EVEN PERCENTAGE * 365
= 33% * 365 = 121 DAYS

From the start of the year, 121 days corresponds to April 30th, which is when COMPANY SUPERTOP technically reached its Break-Even point.

Summary:

Line	Description	2005
1	Net Sales	$1,950,000
2	Cost of Goods Sold	$478,000
3	Total Variable Costs	$178,770
4	Total Fixed Costs	$370,070
5	Net Profit	$923,160
6	L4+(L3/2) = Portion of Total Fixed Costs	$459,455
7	**L7/(L7+L5) = Break-Even %**	**33%**
	Days in Period to Break-Even	121
	Days Per month to Break-Even	10
	Therefore, the Break-Even amounts are:	
	Break-Even for Total Period	**$643,500**
	Monthly	$53,625
	Weekly	$12,375
	Daily	$2,475
	Hourly	$309

Practice:

Calculate the Break-Even amounts and date for COMPANY SUPERTOP for the years of 2006, 2007, and 2008.

Answers:

Line	Description	2006	2007	2008
1	Net Sales	$1,440,000	$2,630,000	$2,920,000
2	Cost of Goods Sold	$397,000	$737,000	$661,000
3	Total Variable Costs	$197,220	$209,710	$221,050
4	Total Fixed Costs	$393,580	$453,140	$483,720
5	**Net Profit**	**$452,200**	**$1,230,150**	**$1,554,230**
6	L4+(L3/2) = Total Fixed Costs	$492,190	$557,995	$594,245
	L7/(L7+L5) = Break-Even %	*~52%	*~31%	*~28%
	Days in Period to Break-Even	190	113	102
	Days Per month to Break-Even	16	9	9
	Therefore Break-Even Amounts Are:			
	Break-Even for Total Period	$748,800	$815,300	$817,600
	Monthly	$62,400	$67,942	$68,133
	Weekly	$14,400	$15,679	$15,723
	Daily	$2,880	$3,136	$3,145
	Hourly	$360	$392	$393

*The Break-Even percentage is an absolute value. It has been rounded up.

Special Case: COMPANY SUPERTOP incurs a loss:

Assume the following in 2005.

Net Sales	$1,200,000
Total Fixed Costs	$850,000
Total Variable Costs	$430,000

Answer:

Net Sales	$1,200,000
Total Fixed Costs	$850,000
Total Variable Costs	*$430,000
Net Profit	-$80,000
Break-Even %	*108%
Break-Even Amount	$1,297,462
Break-Even Date	January 28, 2006

*Remember, we are still adding half of the Variable Costs to the Fixed Costs to get the *Total Fixed Costs.*

Debrief:

The Break-Even percentage is roughly 108%. This means that COMPANY SUPERTOP has incurred a loss because 100% of its sales ($1,200,000) cannot cover its Total Fixed and Variable Costs in 2005. The company needed another $80,000 to Break-Even in 2005 ($1,200,000 — $850,000 — $430,000 = -$80,000). Or, COMPANY SUPERTOP will have to use 8% of the income that will be generated in 2006 to Break-Even in 2005. The extra 8% represents roughly 28 days. *Here, we are holding everything else constant.

TOP

MANAGER

QUIZ:

FIND OUT IF YOU'VE LEARNED ANYTHING!

- ✓ 20 QUESTIONS ONLY (Find the answers on the next section)
- ✓ YOU WILL HAVE TO PICK THE BEST ANSWER FOR SOME QUESTIONS

1. You just joined a new organization, what should be your first priority?

A. Develop new strategies to make the company more profitable
B. Determine who holds the power in the organization
C. Meet with everyone to share your vision
D. Determine the critical areas needed for improvement

2. How do you establish INITIAL credibility as a manager?

A. Ask people targeted questions about the field that concerns them
B. Share your sincere enthusiasm to work with people of all background
C. Make sure that people understand the type of manager you are and plan to be
D. Share your experiences and what you have learned from them

3. When developing a budget, how should you determine the Known-Unknowns (KUs)?

    A. Use the figures from the previous years
    B. Assign probabilities for the likelihood of occurrence of future costs
    C. Use the industry averages
    D. Use your best judgment

4. What makes you DOMINANT in an organization?

    A. Everyone likes you
    B. You control every management meeting
    C. You have the liberty to implement every strategy and idea you have
    D. You don't need to show up at the office everyday

5. How do you avoid debate when presenting your ideas?

    A. Prove to everyone how it has worked perfectly in other places
    B. Be willing to challenge anyone who disagrees with you
    C. Ask people to come up with better ideas
    D. Use your own critical thinking ability to prove your position

6. Why should you avoid "Small Talk"?

    A. It is risky
    B. Everyone does it
    C. It is for lower-level employees
    D. Stating "Small Talks" is not anymore the best way to break the ice

7. How can you better manage the behaviors of those you supervise?

    A. Listen to their concerns and show that you care
    B. Develop good standard procedures
    C. Discover their emotional triggers and refocus their roles more specifically
    D. Become their friend

8. Why being extremely confident is beneficial to the Top Manager?

    A. It means that you are smart
    B. It tells people that you are not intimidated by anyone
    C. It means that you are a good manager
    D. It helps to convince people to follow you when you want to achieve big goals

9. Who should you prioritize first?

    A. Your customers
    B. Your stakeholders
    C. Your employees
    D. Your industry connections

10. What makes the delegation of tasks much easier?

    A. Giving clear direction and guidance
    B. Creating efficient systems and controls
    C. Making people believe that you trust them
    D. Rewarding people if they do well

11. What is the purpose of a Comparative Cost Analysis?

    A. It determines if over-spending has occurred
    B. It outlines the areas of financial success
    C. It explains a company's cost structures
    D. It helps to develop the operational budget

12. What is the purpose of a Z-Score Analysis?

A. It determines the profitability of a company
B. It helps with forecasting
C. It determines the feasibility of the long-term sustainability of a company
D. It compares the gross margins between products

13. What will guarantee long-term sustainability in an organization?

A. Wealth accumulation
B. Many customers and contracts
C. A good management team
D. A good product or service

14. What is the most common pricing strategy used by companies?

A. Differentiation pricing
B. Cost-Plus pricing
C. Penetration Pricing
D. Seasonal Pricing

15. What is the major problem with horizontal organizations?

A. They promote less accountability
B. Employees do not like it
C. They force managers to become more aggressive
D. They create a bad team atmosphere

16. What makes a quality control standard much more effective?

A. If It has lots of back-up plans
B. If It is well understood by everyone
C. If It promotes constant randomness
D. It is easy to follow

17. What is the best tool you can use to determine if a Sales Strategy is effective?

A. Sales Volume
B. Number of customers
C. Market Share
D. Return On Investment (ROI)

18. What is ideally the best type of product to sell regardless of economic downturns?

A. Luxury Products
B. Substitute Products
C. Complement Products
D. Necessity Products

19. Why do most standard procedures fail?

A. They lack a solid control system
B. They are hard to understand
C. They are not updated frequently
D. They don't take into consideration all of the necessary elements of the business

20. What makes cyclical inventory systems so difficult to implement?

A. It requires a lot of staff
B. It requires lot of complicated formulas
C. Staff members do not like it
D. It requires constant discipline and commitment

ANSWERS

1. You just joined a new organization, what should be your first priority?

    A. Develop new strategies to make the company more profitable
    B. Determine who holds the power in the organization
    C. Meet with everyone to share your vision
    D. Determine the critical areas needed for improvement

Answer: B

As a manager, you will always have ideas and strategies. However, without the power to put them into action, you can never accomplish anything. Figure out first who has the power in the organization (i.e.: Board of Directors, "sacred cows", etc.) and develop the necessary strategies to reclaim it before starting to get things done.

2. How do you establish INITIAL credibility as a manager?

    A. Ask people targeted questions about the field that concerns them
    B. Share your sincere enthusiasm to work with people of all backgrounds
    C. Make sure that people understand the type of manager you are and plan to be
    D. Share your experiences and what you learned from them

Answer: A.

Asking people targeted questions about the field that concerns them makes you an expert by default, and therefore credible. Showing too much early excitement may send the signal of a salesperson. Talking about yourself may turn off some people (self-aggrandizing stories are never received well especially when no direct proof is available)

3. When developing a budget, how should you determine the Known-Unknowns (KUs)?

A. Use the figures from the previous years
B. Assign probabilities for the likelihood of occurrence of future costs
C. Use the industry averages
D. Use your -best judgment

Answer: B

The KUs are those costs an organization projects to incur if some situations were to evolve. Essentially, preparing for the KUs is like formulating a backup or contingency plan. There is a distinct uncertainty factor. This is the reason why KUs are budgeted using a **probability system.**

4. What makes you DOMINANT in an organization?

A. Everyone likes you
B. You control every management meeting
C. You have the liberty to implement every strategy and idea you have
D. You don't need to show up at the office everyday

Answer: C

Being dominant means that you have the power to put in action everything you decide and even a Board of Directors cannot stop you. Fear and control will not get everyone to follow your vision willingly. People may just be worried about their paychecks.

5. How do you avoid debate when presenting your ideas?

    A. Prove to everyone how it has worked perfectly in other places
    B. Be willing to challenge anyone who disagrees with you
    C. Ask people to come up with better ideas
    D. Use your own critical thinking ability to prove your position

Answer: D

As a manager, every statement you ever make should be based on and presented as a by-product of your own intellectual prowess. If you open yourself up to hostile challenges and lose, you instantly damage your credibility.

6. Why should you avoid "Small Talk"?

    A. It is risky
    B. Everyone does it
    C. It is for lower-level employees
    D. Starting "Small Talk" is no longer the best way to break the ice

Answer: A

Understandably, you can never make assumptions about people's belief systems, past experiences, general outlook on life, etc. Opening up too much, especially on political, religious, or socio-economic topics, can expose you to condemnation from those with whom you disagree. Think you can keep things inside the boundaries? Think again ... who wants to listen to someone that only talks about the weather?

7. How can you better manage the behaviors of those you supervise?

    A. Listen to their concerns and show that you care
    B. Develop good standard procedures
    C. Discover their emotional triggers and refocus their roles more specifically
    D. Become their friend

Answer: C

In strategic terms, finding this emotional connection attached to someone's career choice will allow you to target your managerial efforts more directly. Accordingly, you would be able to develop a systematic approach to increase their productivity once you have uncovered their ultimate driving force.

8. Why being extremely confident is beneficial to the Top Manager?

    A. It means that you are smart
    B. It tells people that you are not intimidated by anyone
    C. It means that you are a good manager
    D. It helps to convince people to follow you when you want to achieve big goals

Answer D:

For you to achieve great success in any organization, it is essential for every employee to believe that you have the ability to deliver regardless of future contingencies. Everyone should believe that you are the common denominator to success and anybody in your camp will succeed.

9. Who should you prioritize first?

    A. Your customers
    B. Your stakeholders
    C. Your employees
    D. Your industry connections

Answer: C

Great leaders make it as their prime organizational priority to constantly develop their employees. They understand that building an efficient team will ensure long-term growth and success. Instead of focusing solely on attracting the next customer, they will develop enhancement plans necessary to spur the innovative thinking ability of every employee.

10. What makes the delegation of tasks much easier?

    A. Giving clear direction and guidance
    B. Creating efficient systems and controls
    C. Making people believe that you trust them
    D. Rewarding people if they do well

Answer: B

If true systems and controls are in place in an organization, then a leader will be able to delegate full authority to anyone with the confidence that operational activities will be executed at a maximum level of excellence. With efficient Systems and Controls, no one can deviate from the framework regardless of ability and expertise.

11. What is the purpose of a Comparative Cost Analysis?

A. It determines if over-spending has occurred
B. It outlines the areas of financial success
C. It explains a company's cost structures
D. It helps to develop the operational budget

Answer: A

12. What is the purpose of a Z-Score Analysis?

A. It determines the profitability of a company
B. It helps with forecasting
C. It determines the feasibility of the long-term sustainability of a company
D. It compares the gross margins between products

Answer: C

It sheds light on the solvency and the financial strength of a company. In simple terms, the higher the Z-Score, the higher the chances for long-term sustainability. Furthermore, a company with a healthy Z-Score will have less trouble securing funds from financial institutions and venture capitalists. In fact, the Z-Score represents the "Credit Score" of a business.

13. What will guarantee long-term sustainability in an organization?

A. Wealth Accumulation
B. Many customers
C. A good management team
D. A good product or service

Answer: A

Wealth planning should be the central priority for the Top Manager. Every management meeting should begin and end with this concept in mind. Furthermore, a report with a set of recommendations should be produced periodically to assess the wealth status of the organization. If you are not accumulating every week and every month of the year, then any mild storm may seriously compromise your foundation if not putting it into multiple and useless debris.

14. What is the most common pricing strategy used by companies?

A. Differentiation pricing
B. Cost-Plus pricing
C. Penetration Pricing
D. Seasonal Pricing

Answer: B

It simply adds a profit percentage to the cost of production or servicing.

15. What is the major problem with horizontal organizations?

A. They promote less accountability
B. Employees do not like it
C. They force managers to become more aggressive
D. They create a bad team atmosphere

Answer: A

People are less likely to assume responsibility in horizontal organizations because everyone takes on multiple roles at the same time.

16. What makes a quality control standard much more effective?

A. If It has a lot of back-up plans
B. If It is well understood by everyone
C. If It promotes constant randomness
D. It is easy to follow

Answer: C

The basic strategy is to promote constant randomness, which will bear higher success of detecting potential production/servicing errors.

17. What is the best tool you can use to determine if a Sales Strategy is effective?

A. Sales Volume
B. Number of customers
C. Market Share
D. Return On Investment (ROI)

Answer: D

The Return On Investment (ROI) method determines if a strategy is working or needs tweaking. It doesn't matter how much sales you have generated or how many customers you have acquired. What matters is what you have received in return after deducting your investment.

18. What is ideally the best type of product to sell regardless of economic downturns?

    A. Luxury Products
    B. Substitute Products
    C. Complement Products
    D. Necessity Products

Answer: D

They are less sensitive economic shifts and downturns. If a company is selling baby milk for example, then we can assume that its consumer base will always exist. This is the reason why most grocery stores can sustain the harshest economic recessions. However, you should acknowledge that necessity goods bear a low margin. A company must sell large amounts of these goods to remain profitable. In essence, economies of scales (selling many) will solidify profitability.

19. Why do most standard procedures fail?

    A. They lack a solid control system
    B. They are hard to understand
    C. They are not updated frequently
    D. They don't take into consideration all of the necessary elements of the business

Answer: A

Without a control system, standard procedures are meaningless because they amount to a multitude of rules with a limited chance of implementation.

20.   What makes cyclical inventory systems so difficult to implement?

    A. It requires a lot of staff
    B. It requires a lot of complicated formulas
    C. Staff members do not like it
    D. It requires constant discipline and commitment

Answer: D

The cyclical inventory system is difficult to maintain without a certain level of continuity and commitment. Many managers who choose to implement a cyclical system begin with the best of intentions. Then something unexpected happens, and a "temporary" deviation is deemed acceptable in "extenuating" circumstances.

CONCLUSION:

Every Manager is destined to face tough challenges. If you are a newly minted supervisor on the path to becoming Top Manager, ready yourself to acknowledge that these challenges are universal and inevitable. You will deal with difficult employees. You will deal with cyclical downturns and harsh economic realities. You will be confronted at some point in your career with the prospect of failure. What sets the Top Manager apart from the average one is how these challenges are faced. Managing any organization will be tumultuous at best without the right systems, controls, and leadership temperament characteristic of the Top Manager.

This book has outlined the specific steps requisite to becoming a Top Manager.

Mind-Setting...

One becomes a Top Manager by first acquiring an exclusive and disciplined state of mind that establishes instant authority, and control. It is accomplished by not promoting the manager's self-image or extraordinary accomplishments but by instilling immediate credibility with those present in the manager's domain.

True credibility comes only from distinction and results. To achieve this maxim, you must maintain a laser focus on all important issues, and must continue to devise actionable plans to best serve the interests of employees, partners, shareholders and stakeholders, as well as yourself.

This book has given you these tools. Now it is up to you to have the strength of character and unyielding fortitude to ensure these methods are properly carried out. This means confronting those who breach established protocols. It means sending the message to those around you that they are expected to perform tasks at the maximum level of excellence. Anything less will be met with decisive reprimand. With this authority, the Top Manager is able to put in action every plan deemed crucial for the ascension of a company. In like manner, confidence is a great ally to the Top Manager. The Top Manager relies on intellectual and emotional toughness to demonstrate to everyone that no one can do it better.

The Top Manager also understands that prioritizing the continuous professional development of everyone in the organization is paramount to long-term growth and success. Everyone in the organization regardless of title is seen as a vital element to complete the puzzle. Most importantly, the Top Manager is of the mindset that no goal is out of reach, despite the trappings of conventional wisdom. Everyone thought that Climbing Mount Everest was impossible until Sir Edmund Hillary put his name in the history books in 1953. Like many before and after Hillary who have achieved the seemingly impossible. He was told: it simply couldn't be done. It was too dangerous. It was too cold. The aspiration was just too high. The Top Manager is never intimated. The Top Manager seeks to achieve goals that scare the average person. Impossible is relative, and safety an illusion. An airplane may be safe in the hangar, but airplanes were meant to fly. As a Top Manager, so were you. It is the cornerstone of the Top Manager's inner makeup.

Troubleshooting...

Secondly, becoming a Top Manager means that you understand the necessity of auditing and revealing every possible area of inefficiency and to then take swift corrective action before the cracks in the foundation compromise the organization's structural integrity. This book has outlined the most essential tools of a business analysis needed to help mitigate the problems any organization may face. For instance, determining if over-spending has occurred through a Comparative Cost Analysis or dissecting the various snags that exist within a management system through an operational analysis will enlighten the Top Manager about which change-strategies to activate.

Systemizing...

Thirdly, Building the best organizational structure is crucial to facilitating the success of the Top Manager. Any business must be built on a sound foundation. The model introduced throughout this book comprises systems that have proven successful in turning even the most immobilized companies into stellar performers. In fact, this progressive model is the most popular amongst the best consultants in the world. The model begins with the leader cultivating an understanding of which areas necessitate the most urgent attention. These areas are: Planning, Vision, Direction, and Wealth Building. With the targeted focus on these areas, a company can not only have the ability to sustain itself during the harshest economic recession but also increase its chances for long-term sustainability. They help the Top Manager overcome adversity, and to see opportunity in the direst of circumstances.

The model is followed by the installation of strong and efficient systems and controls. If the vision identifies opportunity, systems and controls make the arrival at this point a possibility. The path from the present day to ultimate success is a long journey. As we have discussed throughout this book, systems and controls will allow the Top Manager to keep the company on track. Basically, every task in the organization will be executed with established protocols and the control mechanisms to ensure that they are followed to almost a mathematical certainty.

Next in the Model, we developed a model surrounding personnel management. The outlined structure shows a step-by-step approach to building the best team in any organization. It starts by clearly outlining every job requirement with quantifiable performance metrics, skill enhancement, and adjustment plans. The model then prioritizes the necessity to install strong incentive plans to encourage the constant participation of employees in the organizational success.

Lastly on this model is the obligation to track without fail the Return On Investment (ROI) of every line of business of the company. Furthermore, a contingency plan must be in place and ready to be activated in case the ROI falls to lower than anticipated standards. Since an organization must also seek higher and higher efficiency levels, specific goals to reach these goals must also be in place to consistently increase a company's overall ROIs.

Optimizing...

Lastly, optimizing the core elements of a business will ease the Top Manager's responsibilities if building the best organizational structure is not an immediate goal. These core elements include, for example, flash reports that ease the Top Manager's decision making ability or optimum distribution channels that strategically amplify sales figures.

It is up to you...

So what's next? This book includes an extremely useful collection of the most powerful managerial concepts and techniques. Following these directives will lead any manager on the path to Top Level success. However, this book does not have all the answers. Why? Because as the Top Manager, many of these answers lie inherently within YOU. This book was designed to serve as a guide along your own path of personal Top Manager Discovery. Take some time to implement these practices in your daily management practices. Observe others in their own failure to do so, and note the mistakes and blunders that ensue. Take solace in the fact that these will not be mistakes made by you. Then come back and read this book again. Chances are, the second time around will allow you to learn even more.

Now that you have the blueprint to become a Top Manager, hopefully you will become the next success story. The methods, concepts, and techniques covered in this book have been the driving force behind the success of many other Top Managers in the past, and will continue to be the impetus for honor and accomplishment of many Top Managers to come. It's your turn to take it over the top. Do you have it in you?

www.ingramcontent.com/pod-product-compliance
Lightning Source LLC
Chambersburg PA
CBHW070253200326
41518CB00010B/1774